More Weird Bristol

CHARLIE REVELLE-SMITH

Text copyright © 2019 Charlie Revelle-Smith

All Rights Reserved

For Derek

Introduction: How Did Weird Bristol Come to be?

For years my parents have been coming to visit me in Bristol and every time we will spend a few days walking huge stretches of the city, wandering from my house in Bedminster to the city centre and then it could be up Park Street, or onto Gloucester Road, perhaps Whiteladies Road and then Clifton Village. Whatever route we take, it is always on foot.

One of the greatest things my parents ever taught me and my sister is the joy of a long walk. Growing up in Cornwall we would spend our weekends on long strolls through the countryside or along dramatic clifftops. All the while we were keeping watch for our ever changing surroundings - the first daffodil of spring, the first swallow. A kingfisher or a stoat, a seal or a buzzard.

With this background, you might imagine that I'd be a country mouse forever but when I came to Bristol as a student at UWE in the year 2000, I learned almost overnight that I was actually a town mouse in disguise. I took to urban living at once and embraced the hectic adventure of a city. By day, Bristol was a buzzing metropolis of activity, the likes of which I had never experienced, and by night the city became a debauched celebration of freedom and excess. I loved it all.

But I never stopped walking. Urban walking is, I believe, one of the most underrated activities a person can enjoy and when I do it now, it is with that same eager eye for my surroundings. I'm no longer looking for kingfishers and stoats, but odd pavement engravings and antique lamp posts.

For many years, I had been gathering these bits of trivia, thinking they were of interest only to me but when I came to write to my *Bristol Murders* series, I was able to construct plots around the strange minutiae of Bristol's history. Many of these titbits I uncovered myself but a fair portion of them I owe to my parents who both have masterful eyes for spotting the city's many hidden idiosyncrasies when we go on our long walks.

When I started @WeirdBristol on Twitter in February of 2017, it was essentially just a place to impart some of this peculiar knowledge I'd accrued over the years. I hoped it would find a few followers and maybe might last a few months. Two and half years later it turns out that there's quite an abundance of people who find this kind of strange information interesting - and that has made me enormously surprised and happy to discover!

Writing Weird Bristol - both online and in book form, has been an utter joy. I shall continue with my strange little project until every last corner of this fascinating city has been explored and I hope you will join me on this adventure through the history of this place we call home.

How to Use This Book

Like the first book in this series, *More Weird Bristol* is laid out in a series of walks around our city. However, unlike *Weird Bristol*, where the walks formed one continuous loop around Bristol, this is a little less uniform.

Each walk begins with a map and a brief description of the overall theme or setting. Italicised text will tell you where the walk begins and each subsequent stop will have information on how to get to the next location.

Some of these walks do include a kind of "Choose Your Own Adventure" option. At certain points there are alternative routes which will take you on a detour to another walk so if you're feeling particularly intrepid, you can do several little walks over the course of one larger one. Whenever there is an alternative route, the italicised text will tell you how to get there and also which page to turn to in order to begin that walk.

Of course, there is absolutely no obligation to do any of these walks and you can enjoy this book any way you choose. It doesn't even need to be read cover to cover - you can simply dip in and out of whatever subjects interest you. In fact, I have been told on more than one occasion that my original *Weird Bristol* book has found a permanent home in the bathroom, where it has made perfect "loobrary" reading…

I hope this book informs and entertains you. *More Weird Bristol* will point you in the direction of some of the lesser known history of Bristol, but our city is full of secrets so I hope it also encourages you to discover some of your own!

Walk One
Blaise Castle

Blaise Castle

One of Bristol's best loved treasures can be found in the pretty suburb of Henbury.

Blaise Castle Estate is home not just to the folly which gave the grounds its name, but one of the most stunning gorges to be found in the region.

The first walk in this book is somewhat challenging, with a steep climb to the top of a hill and a long descent into a valley. The section of the walk leading to stop number 8 can also get quite muddy.

This gigantic estate is full of secrets waiting to be discovered and I hope to guide you through some of the more peculiar ones. You will find tales of extinct dogs, a mill that was rescued from a flooded village and a sugar merchant who got his just desserts…

This walk begins at the main entrance to Blaise Castle House on Blaise Castle Estate.

1. Blaise Castle Dogs

Standing either side of the entrance to Blaise Castle House are the statues of two rather peculiar looking dogs. At first glance something seems to be amiss about them - they are far too muscular for any breed we are familiar with - and that is because this breed of dog is now extinct.

The statues are casts of the Jennings Dog, also known as the Dog of Alcibiades, that is thought to date back to the 2nd-century AD and can be found in the British Museum.

The Jennings Dog is itself a replica of a previous statue from about four hundred years earlier and depicts a Molossian Hound from the mountain regions of Greece and Albania. It's believed that these dogs were used for hunting but also as weapons of war, with their tremendous bite strength proving them to be a formidable presence on the battlefield. The statue was lost in AD 69 and the Jennings Dog is thought to be based on descriptions of the original.

The true Molossian Hound became extinct sometime in antiquity, but it's believed that its genetic lineage continues in dogs such as the English Mastiff, Saint Bernard and a number of Greek molosser breeds. In recent years there have been attempts to breed a species which would more closely resemble the hound but these dogs are not regarded as "true" versions of the ancient animal.

One of the statues at Blaise Castle Estate was beheaded in 2007 and evidence in the form of a deep scar around its neck can still be seen. The vandals were never caught but at least the dog was saved to remain a curio for visitors to the estate who may not be aware of the unusual history behind these two sculptures.

The house itself contains a number of 19th century casts of important pieces of art. These include Michelangelo's statue for the tomb of Lorenzo de Medici, while the frieze around the upper walls is taken from the famed (and famously controversial) Elgin marbles.

We're still looking at the house for the next stop, but I recommend heading to its rear so that you can get a good look at the orangery and also a nice tour of the building's exterior.

2. Thomas Farr and John Harford

Too often when we look back on Bristol's history there can be a temptation to assume that the only people engaged in the slave trade were those who were directly profiting from the kidnap and selling of human beings, but the full extent to how local merchants benefited from it is somewhat more complicated.

The earliest mention of what is now Blaise Castle Estate comes from the Domesday Book of 1086 which lists the land as consisting of one square mile, but it's known to have been inhabited even earlier as there are remains of an iron age hill fort on the stretch of ground between Blaise Castle and Kings Weston House.

Thomas Farr bought the land in 1762 and soon set about commissioning a house and landscaping what was at the time a rather dense forest on either side of a steep gorge.

Farr had profited greatly as a sugar merchant and his wealth came from slave labour on plantations in America. In 1776 and the outbreak of the American Revolutionary War, Farr invested greatly in the British Navy, in hopes of securing his business interests into the future, but they were defeated. Farr lost his plantations, was bankrupted and forced to sell his estate.

The current house, which now operates as a fascinating museum of domestic life, was built in 1789 by John Scandrett Harford who replaced the previous one with a grand, neoclassical building complete with an orangery which once would have been filled with exotic plants.

It's during this period that much of the current estate was designed, with famed landscape designer Humphry Repton (who is best remembered as a successor to Capability Brown) laying out much of the park.

The Harford family were noted abolitionists and when John Scandrett Harford Jnr. took over the estate in the early 19th century this tradition continued, with Harford Jnr. hosting prominent people in the fight to end slavery from around the country - one of whom was politician William Wilberforce.

The Slave Trade Act of 1807 prohibited the trade in humans throughout the British Empire, but the Harfords continued to campaign for it to be outlawed across the world. The family owned the house and estate until 1926 when it was bought by Bristol City Council and has been a much-loved public park since 1949.

Our next stop is the castle which gives the estate its name. Depending on the time of year, it can sometimes be spotted among the trees on a hill overlooking the house. As you approach the woodland you will find a path which leads up a steep hill and eventually an opening where the beautiful castle can be found.

3. The Castle

Blaise Castle is a breathtaking marvel and the centrepiece of the estate. Although it is a castle folly, unlike most follies which are purely decorative, it actually served a practical purpose.

It was commissioned by the then estate owner Thomas Farr in 1766, who paid £3,000 for its construction, and was designed by Scottish architect Robert Mylne, who is best known for the original Blackfriars Bridge in London, which at the time of its opening in 1769, was only the third bridge across the Thames in the whole city.

Mylne's bridge was replaced by the current version in 1869 but pictures of his design show a gigantic stone crossing, inspired by Italian architecture and the first bridge in Britain to use elliptical arches.

Mylne's appreciation of rounded forms can be seen in Blaise Castle, with its unusual design featuring a triangle of turrets around a cylindrical keep. The folly was designed in a Gothic Revival style which was hugely popular at the time and was a reimagining of a medieval form, particularly that of ancient churches and castles. The Gothic Revival style was further accentuated with Humphry Repton's 1796 remodelling of parts of the folly's exterior.

Although Farr is thought to have used his folly for entertaining guests (as most follies at the time were used for this purpose), the primary reason for its construction was a financial one.

When the castle was completed Farr had investments in the American sugar trade and had a fleet of ships ferrying the substance which had been so successful it was nicknamed "white gold" by merchants. From his elevated position above his estate, Farr was able to watch his ships arriving and departing Bristol and presumably keep track of their schedules. It also proved to be very popular with visitors to the estate who would pay to see the astonishing views.

The folly is now an icon of the estate and grade II listed as a monument. It opens its doors a few times each summer and I highly recommend a visit as there is a truly spectacular view from the roof all the way out to Avonmouth and the River Severn.

Talking of incredible views, another is very close by. From the castle there is a slight slope downhill which will take you to the edge of a gigantic gorge. This spot is known as Lovers' Leap.

4. Lovers' Leap

In Jane Austen's 1803 novel *Northanger Abbey*, the character of John Thorpe describes Blaise Castle as "the finest place in England - worth going fifty miles at any time to see". Readers have interpreted this as something of an insult to the estate, with the superficial Thorpe being impressed only by showy grandeur and foolishly believing the castle itself to be the oldest in England (it was less than forty years old when Austen wrote her novel).

That said, it's hard to deny that the estate is an exquisite place of beauty, but much like John Thorpe, it has led to people throughout its history embellishing the details to create a romantic mystery about the area.

The spectacular view over the Hazel Brook from the hill on which the castle perches is known as Lovers' Leap and there are rumours that doomed lovers, most likely torn apart by their unsympathetic families, have come to this spot to hurl themselves onto the rocks below so that they might be united in death.

The Georgians particularly had a fondness for naming any dizzying drop a Lovers' Leap and many of them have heart-wrenching, but entirely fictitious, tales of doomed romance and thwarted love.

When the estate was remodelled to the design suggestions of Humphry Repton, it was done so with an eye for romantic drama. In the woods surrounding the spectacular gorge, chimneys were hidden so that a groundskeeper could burn wet wood throughout the day to create an eerie, perpetual mist to shroud the treetops.

Further down the path from the castle there is an artificial cave which was claimed to have been the home of a hermit, but this is probably a fabricated tale too -

and one which likely gave a sense of historic relevance to the grounds.

Blaise Castle is a magnificent treasure, but it's also home to folklore and rumour. The spectacular estate seems to lend itself to grandiose imaginings and throughout its long life, architects and landscapers have sought to emphasise this peculiar topography and turn it into the beautiful but somewhat mysterious place it is today.

We will be going past the hermit's cave as we work our way into the gorge. Follow the steep path down the hill. When you've reached the cave built into the gorge you are about half way down. Continue onwards and take a right turn onto a wider, concrete path which will take you deep into the valley where an old watermill can be found.

5. Stratford Mill

Isolated on a gentle stream and tucked away into the bottom of a deep gorge, Stratford Mill somehow has both a chocolate box beauty and a Hansel and Gretel creepiness about it. It's one of the most prominent and notable buildings on Blaise Castle Estate - which is peculiar, as it was never intended to be here - and is actually the sole surviving building of a village which was intentionally flooded.

The mill was built sometime in the late 18th century and was one of two on a small river which flowed through a picturesque village called Moreton. It served as a flour mill and ownership passed through several generations until the early 1950s when plans were set in motion to flood Moreton along with a couple of hamlets that stood nearby.

The baby boom which followed the second world war led to an unprecedented rise in the national birthrate and the population of cities began swelling at an alarming speed.

Increased car ownership also meant that workers were living farther from city centres, in smaller towns, and Bristol felt this strain as acutely as anywhere else, as houses were built to accommodate a bloating population which was also much more mobile. A major water source had to be secured, and this meant building a reservoir beyond the boundary of Bristol. It was the village of Moreton which would suffer because of it.

There had been suggestions since 1939 that the valley on which Moreton stood would be suitable for a man-made reservoir but by the postwar years it had become an inevitability.

The village stood on what is now Chew Valley Lake and was home to some very pretty and historic buildings, but Stratford Mill, with its pink pennant stone bricks and homely appearance, was the only building judged worthy of saving and it was moved brick by brick, along with its machinery, into Blaise Castle Estate, where it made a delightful addition to the gorge.

The rest of Moreton was not quite so lucky. Most of the buildings were demolished and the residents moved to a purpose-built village. An ancient stone cross was moved from the local church's grounds, but the building itself was demolished.

On summer days, when the water level of the enormous reservoir can drop by several feet, it's still possible to see bits of wall, field boundaries and the stone cores of medieval hedgerows. At one end of the lake there is even a section of road which leads straight into the water.

When Stratford Mill was moved, it may have inadvertently brought an unexpected guest along with it, as it is claimed that the ghost of a young woman who drowned in the water beside the mill started appearing in Blaise Castle soon after the building was rebuilt.

She is said to be wearing Victorian clothes and stands by the edge of water, perhaps warning visitors to the mill of the danger she succumbed to.

Follow the course of the river over a charming bridge and head deeper into the gorge. You have a terrific vantage point of the limestone walls on either side and the geology of this area is the focus of our next stop.

6. Hazel Brook

The spectacular gorge which divides Blaise Castle Estate was created over millennia by the Hazel Brook, a tributary of the River Trym.

To see the gentle flow of water it may seem unlikely that this vast gorge could be carved by little more than a stream but that is precisely what happened. It's quite possible that it was formed around the same time as the Avon Gorge and that both magnificent formations were caused by the ice age, when a glacier which covered much of England forced waterways to alter their routes.

If true, this probably means that the Hazel Brook was once considerably larger and faster flowing. The brook begins by Cribbs Causeway and meanders through Blaise Castle towards Coombe Dingle, where it forms a delightful valley walk before rejoining the main course of the Trym.

The gorge at Blaise Castle, with its sheer limestone edifices on either side is, to my mind, easily the equal of Cheddar Gorge - and has not suffered from the influx of tourists which make that village so overcrowded at times.

It seems that progressive generations of estate owners have chosen to keep the gorge to themselves so as not to spoil its natural beauty and it has remained relatively the same even after Blaise Castle became a public park in 1949 - with many visitors completely unaware that the discretely hidden gorge even exists.

Even if they chose not to capitalise on the striking formation financially, it seems that members of the Harford family would take guests through the meandering valley in a horse and cart, to impress them upon arrival at the estate.

The Hazel Brook is little more than a thin stream on most days but the stunning gorge it carved is a beautiful reminder of the staggering permanence of geology. It will remain one of Bristol's finest natural treasures.

Keep following the river until it reaches a manmade lake/pond. Facing down the river you should be able to see two huge towers of stone jutting from the left side of the gorge.

7. Goram's Chair

Bristol may be known for many things, but folklore isn't one of them. Compared to other parts of the country - including most of the west and southwest of England, it has a surprising dearth of myths about itself - but it does have Goram and Ghyston/Vincent, even if their tale isn't strictly speaking true folklore.

High above the gorge at Blaise Castle is Goram's chair, a pair of dense ridges that rise ominously from the rock face. It's the kind of geographical feature that is so striking, it was destined to have tales told about it.

The oft-repeated story of Goram and Ghyston usually follows these lines. Two giant brothers live above a huge lake which covers the land from Bristol to Bradford-on-Avon. One day they are tasked by a beautiful maiden named Avona to drain the lake so that a city can be built upon the ground.

Ghyston found success by breaking through the rock to make the Avon Gorge while Goram did the same at Henbury, but grew tired and fell asleep in his chair - Goram's chair in Blaise Castle Estate. When he awoke, Ghyston has succeeded and the maiden Avona was betrothed to him. Goram hurled himself into the Bristol Channel and drowned.

Although the origins of this tale go all the way back to the 16th century, there's a reason why it's regarded as more faux than folklore by collectors of such tales and that is because it was never meant to be believed.

Unlike tales of fairies snatching children in East Anglia, devilish imps terrorising miners in Cornwall or the horrifying water kelpie of Scotland, which were intended to convince an audience of their literal reality, the story of Goram and Ghyston is part of a genre of tales which are entirely fictional and intended to be believed as such.

Much like Rudyard Kipling's *Just-So Stories*, the myth is simply an interesting but somewhat bizarre tale woven around geographical features that can be found around the Bristol area.

Still, it's a charming if sad tale of the perils of laziness, and for centuries people have been imagining poor Goram asleep in his chair overlooking the magnificent gorge.

A bit of backtracking is necessary now. Retrace your steps to the watermill and follow the path to the right of it, heading parallel to the river. Eventually you will come to a small bridge which leads over the river and after that, a tunnel beneath a residential garden. You will emerge in the grounds of St Mary's Church and nearby you will see a beautiful gravestone shaped like an obelisk and an ankh laid out on the ground.

8. Amelia Edwards

The extraordinary memorial of an obelisk and ankh in the churchyard of St Mary's, Henbury is the final resting place of Amelia Edwards - a pioneering travel writer and campaigner for archaeological preservation, with a particular interest in Egyptology.

Born Amelia Ann Blanford Edwards in London, 1831, Edwards was one of those creative youths who had an enthusiastic devotion to the arts but not really a fixed idea of which medium should express that spark.

She embraced writing and poetry alongside composing music and painting. She even branched into caricatures but never thought any of these were her true calling. It did not help that her father was vehemently opposed to his daughter pursuing a career in the arts and did everything within his power to prevent her from doing so.

Nevertheless, Edwards settled on writing and had soon published a handful of mildly successful novels. Of these, *Barbara's History* is possibly the most well read, but I would recommend her novella *The Phantom Coach* for being genuinely eerie.

It was not until 1873 that Edwards discovered her true calling when she and a handful of friends set off for Egypt for several months. This was fairly scandalous as Edwards was unmarried and travelling with a mixed-sex group of people.

The resulting book from her adventure, *A Thousand Miles up the Nile,* was an instant success and her 1891 follow up, *Pharaohs, Fellahs and Explorers,* cemented her status as a travel writer of great warmth and wit.

It was in her later years that Edwards became an advocate for the preservation of ancient relics, after hearing that tourists were often travelling to Egypt and pilfering burial chambers of their goods. It was a campaign she continued until her death in 1892.

Amelia Edwards was a pioneer in more ways than one. Though she never married, she is known to have had several relationships with both men and women, the most significant of which was with Ellen Drew Braysher who she lived with. Astonishingly, her partner is buried alongside her in this beautiful grave - which was such a rarity for the time that Historic England has awarded this memorial a Grade II listing for its importance to LGBT+ history.

We're staying in the graveyard for the next stop. At the front entrance to the church there are a pair of ornate and brightly painted headstones marking a grave.

9. Scipio Africanus

Amelia Edwards is not the only notable person to have been buried in the grounds of St Mary's, Henbury as the graveyard contains one of the most famous graves in Bristol, that of Scipio Africanus (1702-1720).

The significance of this grave has more to do with what the young man represents than who he actually was, as we know almost nothing about him, including his real name as he was a slave, and had presumably been named after a Roman general by one of his masters.

The only things we can say for sure about him is that he worked as a manservant for the Earl of Suffolk, who lived in Henbury, and that he died aged only 18. What his living conditions were like or how he was treated can never be known.

Because Bristol was so heavily involved in the slave trade, it's often assumed that the city must have had a disproportionate number of slaves among its population during the 18th century, but this doesn't seem to be the case. Of those who did live in the city, virtually nothing is known about them.

It's also often thought that the head and foot stones marking the grave of Scipio Africanus are so ornate that they must reflect the fondness with which he was treated by his "master" but this was actually a rather plain memorial originally.

The colour was not added until the 20th century and the foot stone was added in the 1850s. The foot stone itself makes for quite uncomfortable reading for modern eyes, detailing as it does Scipio's "glorious" transformation into a Christian and juxtaposing the darkness of his skin with the light of the Lord. However, this stone was actually installed by 19th century anti-slavery campaigners.

Although slavery had been abolished by the 1850s in the UK, there was still a movement within the country to have it outlawed across the world. Campaigners sought to sway public opinion in Britain by pointing out that Africans could be civilised and even Christian. It may feel like a premise that's distastefully colonialist nowadays, but, shockingly, this was a time where much of the western world wasn't completely sure if black people were even truly human.

The grave of Scipio Africanus is a sombre memorial to a stranger and though he lived for only 18 years, his significance to British history will hopefully never be forgotten.

Leave the churchyard via the gate onto Church Lane. Follow it left until it reaches Kings Weston Road and then take a right onto Hallen Road. The first turning on the left will take you into Blaise Hamlet.

10. Blaise Hamlet

Blaise Hamlet is a quaint collection of nine cottages around a green. Each cottage is stylised in a different, yet adorably English fashion and the green itself is completed with a charming sundial.

The hamlet was commissioned by John Scandrett Harford in 1809 and finished two years later to a design by John Nash, whose most famous achievements are Buckingham Palace and Marble Arch.

The cottages were to house the retired workers who had served the Harford family. This was no small act of charity as it would have ensured that the former workers would be protected for the rest of their lives. John Harford was a noted philanthropist and invested a great deal of his money in charitable causes, especially ones aimed at helping the poor.

The hamlet is now regarded as the first ever example of a garden suburb. The concept behind such design is that of a small village on the outskirts of a city which serves as its own self-contained community. This later became thought of as the antithesis of the green city concept, where urban centres are ringed off by greenbelts.

John Nash was selected as the designer of the hamlet as he was a master of the popular Picturesque design movement. Picturesque aimed to create the aesthetic ideal and borrowed from a number of architectural and artistic styles to create a final product which celebrates beauty and the sublime above all else.

Then, just as now, the Picturesque movement had its detractors. Blaise Hamlet has often been accused of being Harford and Nash's attempt to recreate a version of England that never existed - or at least, was by 1809 hugely outdated. Others have suggested that the hamlet is excessively quaint and almost sickly sweet in its overindulgence.

The nine cottages are, in house number order, Oak Cottage, Diamond Cottage (often singled out as being the epitome of the Picturesque style), Dutch Cottage, Double Cottage (which, as the name suggests is actually two cottages), Rose Cottage, Dial Cottage (the one closest to the sundial, of course), Circular Cottage, Sweetbriar Cottage and Vine Cottage. All of these homes have remained almost constantly occupied, but Rose Cottage has recently become a holiday let.

Whatever your personal thoughts on the Picturesque style, it's hard to deny that this little hamlet is a remarkable addition to both Henbury and Blaise Castle.

That is the end of this walk around Blaise Castle Estate. It's always a lovely place to while away a few hours and I also highly recommend the fascinating museum in Blaise Castle House.

Walk Two
Around The Harbour
(Part One)

Around the Harbour (Part One)

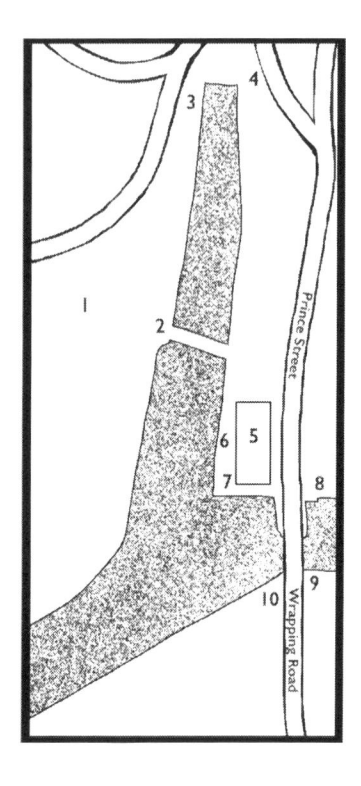

The second walk in this tour is a casual stroll around the harbourside. The harbour is dense with history so I've decided to split this walk into two parts, the first of which is mainly focused on Bristol's history of industry and manufacturing. This walk is very simple and includes an optional and slightly more challenging detour at the third stop.

On this walk we will encounter - among other things - an intrepid explorer, a Caribbean slave and a cold blooded murder that shocked and divided the city…

Our walk begins outside We The Curious where there is an enormous chimney towering over the square.

1. The Anchor Square Chimney

Anchor Square is the charming open space between Pero's Bridge and Millennium Square, which is home to We The Curious and the Bristol Aquarium. Its most eccentric feature may be 1999 sculpture by Nicola Hicks of a fantastical hybrid of a rhinoceros beetle and a stag beetle, which was commissioned as part of a massive regeneration project that began in the late '90s.

It is a curious quirk of urban living that once commutes or casual walks become familiar, we can stop seeing some of the most obvious and conspicuous architecture of a city and such is the case with the gigantic chimney which towers over the square - a testament to Bristol's industrial past which too often seems to go unnoticed.

The chimney, along with the adjoining building which is now a restaurant, was built in 1884 and was once part of a larger factory which stood on this spot. The factory belonged to Rowe Brothers Lead Works and served the purpose of lead rolling, a process where highly heated metal is passed through pairs of rotating rolling pin-like contraptions at enormous pressure until the metal is both reduced in thickness and uniform along its surface.

It can be hard to imagine now, but the whole area of the harbourside was once a thriving hub of industrial activity. Towards the final quarter of the Victorian era, the largest industries were boat building and metalwork (often working alongside one another) but for a long time before then the city had thrived on the manufacturing of glassware.

By the end of the 19th century, the harbour was dense with factories, most with tall chimneys such as this one, belching out black smoke that would turn the sky above Bristol grey on windless days. Factories and warehouses dwindled in number by the 1970s as the harbour ceased to operate commercially (the Avonmouth Docks having grown in scale and usage) and eventually the last of these industrial buildings locked its gates for the final time.

The Rowe Brothers Lead Works remained empty and unused for many decades, and though much of the labyrinth of old factories were levelled, the building managed to survive into the 1990s, when a regeneration programme aimed to clear much of the neglected areas of the harbour and turn former industrial spaces into ones for leisure. Since then, the waterways have been lined with bars, nightclubs, galleries and museums, turning the fortunes of the city around and forging a new identity for Bristol as a destination spot for a night out and as a tourist attraction in its own right.

The Anchor Square chimney is one of the few reminders of the city's industrial heritage which can be found along the harbourside and it serves as an important link between the city's past, its present - and as long as it continues to stand high above the square - its future.

Our next destination is Pero's Bridge, the unmistakable and quirky bridge across the water which can be easily seen from Anchor Square.

2. Pero's Bridge

Pero's Bridge was opened in 1999 and was part of the large-scale rejuvenation project which would also see the construction of Millennium Square. Its purpose was to offer visitors to Queen Square quick and easy access to the stretch of old warehouses which were to become eateries and bars, as well as the new developments which were being built at the time.

The bridge is a bascule bridge - a kind of drawbridge which relies on counterweights to allow its 11 metre span to fully open, allowing large vessels access to the far end of St Augustine's Reach. Despite it being mandated that the bridge must have the capability to open, it performs this task so infrequently that most Bristolians have never seen it in operation.

The bridge's most noticeable feature are the two enormous horns which loom over it. These were designed by Irish sculptor Eilis O'Connell and serve the dual purpose of being both an eye-catching art piece and also a counterweight for the bridge's lifting mechanism.

In recent years, the bridge has become adorned with "love-locks", padlocks bolted to the metalwork by couples, who then toss the key into the water below in hopes that their relationship will be as permanent as the unmovable lock itself. It's a controversial tradition, not least of all in Paris where it is thought to have begun. Until 2015, when they were removed with industrial bolt cutters, over nine tons of padlocks were cut from the Point des Arts bridge, for fear that the additional weight was compromising the integrity of the structure.

The bridge takes its name from Pero Jones, often known simply as Pero, an enslaved man from the small island of Nevis in the West Indies. Little is known of Pero's early life but it's believed that he was sold into slavery aged 12, along with two of his siblings and that he came to Bristol in 1784, aged about 30, where he was forced into servitude for John Pinney, a sugar plantation owner who was also one of the richest men in Bristol at the time.

Many plantation owners during the latter part of the 18th century were often unaware of (or turned a blind eye to) their involvement in the slave trade, but Pinney had no such qualms. Being a vocal advocate for both slavery and for the supremacy of the white race above all others. Despite the city's association with the slave trade, there were only a few slaves known to have been kept in Bristol itself, but John Pinney eventually came to "own" Pero, who worked as he personal servant, as well as Frances Coker, a freed slave who served as lady's maid to his wife.

Pero lived in the building which is now the Georgian House Museum on Great George Street, which houses a small display on what historical detail remains on Pero's life. Pero died around 1798, by which time he had taken heavily to drink. It is believed that John Pinney never gave him his freedom and that Pero died a slave.

Facing Pero's Bridge from the Anchor Square side, turn left and follow the walkways beneath the overhang until you reach the end. At the water's edge, you should be able to see a grated opening beside Cascade Steps.

3. St Augustine's Reach

The stretch of water which begins opposite M-Shed and travels under Pero's bridge until it meets Cascade Steps is known as St Augustine's Reach. It was once lined on either side with shipbuilding warehouses and industrial units but is now a bustling and lively quarter of award winning restaurants and bars.

Although the current waterway was constructed along with the rest of the Floating Harbour in 1809, astonishingly, St Augustine's Reach was first carved during the 1240s, when workers laboured for years to dig a deep, broad trench which would connect the River Avon to the River Frome, which had been artificially diverted through the city (partly to form a moat around Bristol Castle, that stood where Castle Park can now be found).

This incredible feat of engineering was dug entirely by hand (unlike the New Cut, which also used explosives to clear a way through larger rocks) and must have been a truly back-breaking task for those involved.

With the two rivers now connected, St Augustine's Reach became the central heart of Bristol and would help cement the city's reputation as one of the most important docks in the country. By the 18th century, Bristol was second only to London as a city of international trade and it was claimed that the harbour was so dense with ships it was possible to cross from one side to another across their decks.

Most of the Frome has now been covered over to allow for expansion of the city, but there is one small fragment of history that is a reminder of that incredible 13th century achievement. At the water's edge beside Cascade Steps there is a grate built into the harbour wall, through here is the diverted channel through which the River Frome connects to the harbour. Though greatly expanded on during the Victorian era, sections of the underground waterway may date back to the original channel which was dug through the city.

It is possible to follow the river through tight tunnels and over weirs to both Castle Park and the Feeder Canal and it is occasionally attempted by intrepid canoeists. It's a little known fact that over 60km of artificial waterways flow beneath the streets of Bristol.

One thing that's also worth pointing out - not because it's particularly unusual, but because it's vital that every Bristolian is aware of its existence - is the "life-chain" which can be easily spotted along the waterline from this point. The life-chain runs for miles around the harbour and offers those unlucky souls who find themselves having fallen into the water something to cling to until help arrives.

Remember the life-chain and tell your friends about it. It's an unfortunate reality that the harbour has claimed countless victims over the centuries, but this simple chain has offered help to those who have needed it most.

Walk around Cascade Steps until you reach an unusual looking fountain bearing the likeness of two workers on one side and a lion's head on the other (an explanation for this unlikely fountain can be found in my first Weird Bristol Book).

At this point in the walk there are alternate routes if you are in the mood for a diversion. If you would like to explore the history of College Green, head up Park Street to the Marriott Hotel and turn to page 115, or if you'd like an adventure through central Bristol, head to the Hippodrome and turn to page 87.

4. The Narrow Quay Murder

No city can be immune from violence, but Bristol has had more than its fair share of grisly murders over the centuries. One particularly memorable incident occurred close to where the King George V memorial fountain can now be found on Narrow Quay in 1875.

The cobbled street which follows St Augustine's Reach was once dense with doss houses and tenements. Often multiple generations of families would share a single, squalid room. One couple who lived along the quay were Catherine and Philip Morris, both aged 39.

Catherine found occasional work as a tailor and seamstress while her husband was a retired soldier who lived on an army pension. The pair were alcoholics and notoriously violent drunks. In an area known for frequent, drunken brawls and every vice known to man (sailors coming into dock would be enticed by sex workers, gambling and even drugs,) to stand out as troubled drinkers was quite an achievement in itself.

The sensational crime began with the Morris' neighbours hearing screams from the room above them and, after breaking in the door, found Catherine Morris unconscious on the floor in a pool of her own blood. Philip coolly informed his neighbour that he had bludgeoned his wife repeatedly with a tailoring board following a drunken fight and that he would go to the police at once to confess.

Philip was kept in a cell overnight and the following morning he was informed that his wife had miraculously survived the night. Despite having mostly sobered up from the drink, Philip did not take kindly to this news and exclaimed "If she's not dead now, I'll dead her next time!"

Catherine would go on to die from her injuries later that morning and Philip was arrested for her murder. It is that this point that the story takes an unexpected and grotesque turn. Word soon spread that Catherine had not only been married before but had two children out of wedlock. Moreover, she was described as a scold and a shrew, with a fierce temper and a vicious tongue.

A great many people of this time were quite comfortable in blaming the victim for her own murder and by the time Philip Morris' trial began, a petition asking for leniency for the spousal murderer had over 15,000 signatures.

The hypocrisy of the Victorian era has been well documented, but it's still shocking to hear that in his summation of the crime, the judge offered nothing but sympathy for Philip in having tolerated his wife's indecency and drunkenness for so many years. Despite being found guilty, Philip was spared the gallows and was wished the best of luck before he was extradited to Australia as a convict.

The tragic case of Catherine Morris remains a dark and disturbing chapter in the history of Bristol, not just because of the ghastly way in which she was murdered, but for the double standards which led to many people of the city siding with a violent, drunken murderer over the victim herself.

Follow the quay past the other side of Pero's Bridge and then onward to the Arnolfini - the large, handsome building overlooking the harbour.

5. The Arnolfini

The Arnolfini is a contemporary arts centre which has forged a reputation for bold exhibitions from world-class artists. From the outside, it can be hard to fully appreciate the sheer scale of the building but wandering through the many exhibition spaces and studios it becomes clear just how deceptively vast this construction is.

The first stage of what is now the Arnolfini was completed in 1831 and with the addition of a large extension in 1836, it became one of the largest non-religious buildings in the city. Initially, it was built as a warehouse for the iron foundry D.,E. & A. Acraman. The warehouse was named Bush House and designed by Richard Shackleton, using stone sourced from Bath and south Wales. At the time, it's unlikely that Shackleton could have had any idea how influential his design would prove to be.

Shackleton drew attention to features of his design by highlighting them in sandstone which would have contrasted very strongly against the grey pennant stone when the building was new. This effect is most noticeable around the arched windows and entranceways and is likely to have been influenced by similar motifs on Moorish and Byzantine architecture.

Bristol Byzantine, the architectural style which would come to define Bristol throughout the mid-19th century is believed to have taken direct inspiration from Shackleton's Bush House. The style pushed the contrast between brick types even further - and no greater surviving example can be found than that of the Granary on Welshback, which is a glorious, intricate celebration of excess.

From about 1850 to the 1880s, barely a single building was built in any other style in the city, yet almost almost overnight, the faddish Victorians moved onto the next fashionable concept and the style was abandoned.

Bush House served as an iron foundry warehouse for only a few decades before it was repurposed to store tea. It was actually not the first location for the Arnolfini to call home, but the third. Jeremy Rees founded the establishment in 1961 in Clifton and then later in Queen Square. So popular was the art space it soon became apparent that a larger venue was needed and by 1975, the warehouse became available.

The unusual name for the Arnolfini comes from Jan van Eyck's mesmerising 1434 oil painting *The Arnolfini Wedding*, which features a mind-bending effect where the artist himself is reflected in a concave mirror against the far wall of the painting. Jeremy Rees used this painting as inspiration for how he hoped his arts centre would hold a mirror up to artists themselves.

Since establishing itself at Bush House, the Arnolfini has become one of the most daring, provocative and well-loved institutions in all of the city.

From the Arnolfini entrance it is a simple stroll to the next stop on this walk. At the water's edge you will be close to where a very strange incident happened in Bristol almost 250 years ago.

6. The Bristol Arsonist

A 1760 painting of Broad Quay that's often attributed Philip Vandyke (and is now part of M-Shed's display collection) depicts the area around St Augustine's Reach as a buzzing hive of activity with sailors and merchants thronging the streets and the water dense with boats. It's believed that this painting was probably quite accurate to Bristol in its heyday as a major port.

Just seventeen years later, the area depicted in this painting would be the subject of one of the most bizarre crimes in the history of the city.

in 1777, 25 year old James Hill arrived in Bristol with a devious yet inexplicable plan - to burn the docks to ashes. Whether or not the reason for the compulsion was known even to him will remain a mystery, but the man was determined - and seemingly unstoppable.

On a winter's night he crept aboard three ships moored in the harbour. The ships were Hibernia, La Fame and Savannah La Mar and over each he poured turpentine and pitch before setting them ablaze. Of the three vessels, only Savannah La Mar was seriously damaged and the fires were quickly extinguished before they could spread further along the docks.

No doubt frustrated by his unquenched thirst for fire, Hill was out again the next night, attacking warehouses on the harbourside. These wooden buildings were quick to burn and the fire caught on quickly - claiming several properties including homes but there were no reported injuries.

The following morning it was apparent this had been no accident and a reward of £500 was offered to anyone who could catch the culprit - a figure which later doubled. It was at this point that Hill realised that he had to flee the city and paid for his passage to Dover. Soon after his arrival, he was arrested.

The sensational details of the man's crimes spread throughout the country. Soon it was revealed that not only was James Hill a much feared highwayman who had escaped the clutches of the law for years, but that he had attempted to destroy docks in Chatham, Plymouth and Portsmouth as well as Bristol.

Following a speedy trial, Hill was found guilty and sentenced to death. He was brought to Portsmouth jail, close to the scene of his first arson attack and hanged from a ship's mast which had been erected in front of the gates where a huge crowd had formed to watch the execution.

James Hill's bizarre crimewave is an act which defies explanation and though his reasons for wanting watch cities burn to the ground may have died with him, we can at least thank his incompetence for having saved Bristol's beloved docks.

At the corner of St Augustine's Reach and the main channel of the Floating Harbour, there is a forlorn statue of a man staring out at the water. This man is John Cabot and he will be the subject of our next stop.

7. The Cabot Statue

Stephen Joyce's 1985 statue of John Cabot bears a forlorn, almost sad expression as the explorer gazes wistfully out across the harbour. A persistent rumour claims that the statue was aligned so that he would forever be looking in the direction of Newfoundland in Canada, where it's believed his ship first grounded after crossing the ocean, but in actuality he is facing in the direction of Nicaragua.

Another claim often made about John Cabot is that he was the first person to set foot upon the continent of North America (Christopher Columbus having only made it as far as the Caribbean in his 1492 voyage). Aside from neglecting the fact that the continent was already inhabited by millions of people, who had established their own cultures and languages, Cabot cannot even lay claim to being the first European, as the Vikings are thought to have started exploring the "New World" as early as the 12th century.

However, Cabot certainly was the first European in hundreds of years to make it across the Atlantic to mainland America, and that feat in itself is no small achievement.

He was born around 1450 in the Italian city of Genoa. At birth he was given the name of Giovanni Caboto, but when he came to live in England, he anglicised his name to John Cabot. In 1497 he set sail from Bristol aboard his ship the Matthew with a small crew and hopes that, he would find a passage to India over the western horizon, rather than having to travel the laborious and treacherous journey west.

Aboard his ship was explorer William Weston, a Bristol merchant and explorer who lived on Corn Street.

Weston's name should be better known among Bristolians, as this man became the first Briton ever to set foot on American soil.

Although Cabot was celebrated upon his return to the city, the voyage was seen by many as a disappointment. Not only had he failed to find an alternative route to India, but he had not returned with any exotic goods from across the seas. Although he had not met any of the inhabitants from the strange new land, he reported that he had seen evidence of human occupation.

The following year, Cabot returned to the sea for a second voyage to America. It is on this journey that he seems to get lost to history, with many presuming that he and his crew were drowned in the Atlantic. Other theories suggest that the explorer returned and moved to London by 1500 where he died of the plague, while another, rather fanciful one has Cabot living among the natives of the New World - a theory based on seemingly no evidence whatsoever.

Whatever Cabot's final fate was will likely remain a mystery and though many stories of his life may have been greatly exaggerated, or downright inaccurate, there is no denying that his fascinating life and achievements are one of the most significant stories from Bristol history.

Head towards Prince Street Bridge. On this side of the harbour there is a small, iron crane. Head here for the next stop on the walk.

8. The Hand Crane

Beside Prince Street stands a handsome relic from the Victorian era that is almost hiding in plain sight. Not as majestically tall as the massive cranes alongside M-Shed or as unique as the Fairbairn crane, this humble but miraculous hand-cranked crane is often unfairly overlooked, but when it was first constructed, it was regarded as one of the mechanical marvels of the harbourside.

The crane was built in 1886 and was, and still is, capable of hauling a little over a ton in weight. Thanks to an ingenious pulley system, it can perform this feat using the strength of only one man.

Unlike the bigger cranes which were owned by large-scale companies, this crane often served as a business venture in its own right, with people paying to hire the contraption for smaller assignments coming in and out of Bristol.

By the 1930s, hand cranked cranes such as this one were found all around the harbour, catering to the needs of vessels with lighter loads. The operation could be performed quickly and relatively inexpensively.

Another example of a similar crane can be found on Phoenix Wharf, close to the entrance to the Redcliffe Caves and just around the corner from the Ostrich Inn. This crane could carry a similar load but is made mostly from wood. It's well worth a visit as it is the only intact, operation wooden crane left in the city.

These charming little cranes are reminders of the importance Bristol once served as a port of international significance, with goods arriving and departing with the rise and fall of each tide, and though they might not be quite as spectacular as the lofty giants across the water, it's wonderful that they've been preserved as part of our heritage.

The next stop on this walk is… well, you're pretty much there already, as it's Prince Street Bridge. I suggest crossing on the left side of the bridge as you face it from the hand-crane (be careful, as this side has traffic on it) to the spot at the far side where you can see a circular wooden structure in the water.

9. Prince Street Bridge

Anyone who has lived south of Bristol harbour can relate to the frustration of a Prince Street Bridge swing. Somehow the swing always seems to coincide with mornings when you're already late for work or in a rush to get somewhere. The swing itself is actually powered by a rather elegant piece of design which has served the city for 140 years.

The bridge was built in 1879, along with the two cream-coloured buildings beside it. The shorter of these two is an engine house while the taller is an accumulator, which uses heavy weights to pressurise water through narrow tubes. The force of this water is capable of shifting incredible amounts of weight and it is this energy which is harnessed to swing the bridge back and forth.

On the Redcliffe side of the bridge and at the water level, a semi circle constructed from wood can be seen. Although it's often assumed that this must have something to do with operating the bridge swing, it is, rather surprisingly, the remains of a police station which was once built into the harbour.

The station was for a division of the Bristol constabulary, who patrolled the waterways in and around Bristol by boat, apprehending miscreants who had broken the byelaws on the water.

The station was a rather simple structure, with a single story built on stilts over a small jetty where motorboats were moored and could be quickly accessed at the first signs of trouble.

As can be seen by the footprint of its foundations in the water, the police station was rather small and cramped and by 1954 it was beginning to look rather weather beaten and damp. The building was dismantled and a new one was built over the slipway at what is now the Riverstation pub and restaurant. This slipway itself was once an ancient crossing of the harbour, with a hidden ridge beneath the water allowing farmers access to either side of the river at low tide.

In 2015, urgent repairs meant that a temporary footbridge had to be constructed from scaffolding to allow people to cross the harbour. The repairs were expected to take only six months and cost less than half a million but when the full extent of the corrosion to the bridge was revealed, the cost almost tripled and the repairs took close to two years. As frustrating as this was at the time, it ensured that our lovely little historic bridge could be preserved - and remain in operation, for many years to come.

Across the street, towards M-Shed you will see a series a train tracks embedded in the ground. If you're lucky, it might even be a day where the steam locomotives are in operation. These tracks are the focus of our next stop.

10. Trains

The familiar sight of steam trains chugging along the harbourside, pushing or pulling carriages full of people from M-Shed to SS Great Britain has become such a feature of summer in Bristol, that it never really feels like the season has truly started until you hear that welcome blast of a steam whistle for the first time in the year.

Though the trains are mainly used for pleasure trips nowadays, the railway tracks which weave along the harbour played a vital role in Bristol's industrial past. The existing railway (not to be confused with the nearby tracks which are used to move the cranes about) were first laid down in 1872 as a means to quickly transport goods from ships coming into port to Temple Meads railway station where they could then be dispatched to locations around the country.

Laying these tracks was no small feat as, although Temple Meads is not geographically far away, the most direct route would pass directly through St Mary Redcliffe churchyard.

As always, the industrious Victorians had a grand-scale plan. They would dig underneath the church and the churchyard so that trains could pass beneath it, leaving the holy building intact. Evidence of the quarter mile tunnel (which was dug mostly by hand using pickaxes) can be found between the Bathurst Basin end of Guinea Street and the Ostrich Inn, where a boarded up tunnel entrance can be found in the far wall of a small carpark.

The train line became so popular that it was soon extended as far west as the dry dock where the SS Great

Britain was built and was capable of processing dozens of ships' cargos every day.

It's sometimes assumed that the steam locomotives which operate today are historic replicas but they are both genuine relics from the past.

The green engine, named Henbury, was built in 1937 and was put to work at Avonmouth, ferrying goods about the docks. Henbury was one of many similar locomotives performing this operation and they continued working until the 1960s when diesel powered engines superseded them.

They grey engine, Portbury, is even older. Built in 1917, it is one of the oldest industrial steam locomotives still operating in Britain. It was built for a similar purpose to Henbury but with the outbreak of WWI was repurposed to assist in constructing the Portbury docks, which would play an important role in the war effort - and would be where this charming little engine would get its name.

That's the end of the first part of this tour around the harbourside. To continue onto the second half of the walk, which focuses more on Bristol's history as a seafaring city, the first stop will be the huge cranes that can be found outside the M-Shed and should be towering over your head from where you stand now.

Walk Three
Around The Harbour
(Part Two)

Around the Harbour (Part Two)

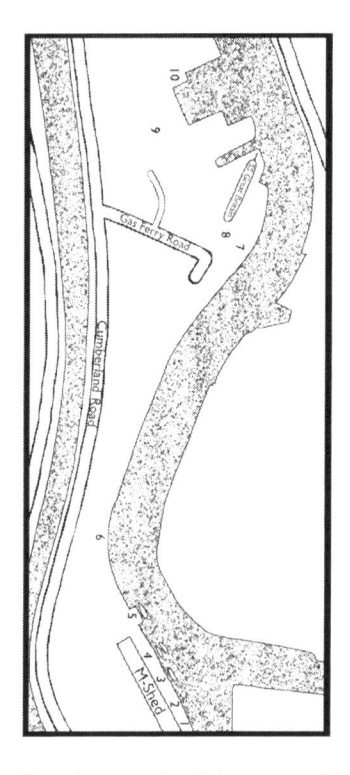

We're heading for the sea in this second half of an exploration of Bristol Harbour.

The historic and beautiful docks have witnessed extraordinary events over the years and we'll be touching on some of the most significant - and unusual - including the campaign which helped save our magnificent cranes, an epic journey which changed the course of history and the world's most mysterious artist...

This Walk begins beneath the enormous cranes outside of M-Shed.

1. Saving the Cranes

Towering above the harbour like huge, metallic dinosaurs, the four electric cranes outside M-Shed are one of the most familiar sights in central Bristol. As well-loved and evocative of the city's past as they are, it's astonishing to think that we almost lost these beautiful landmarks altogether.

Of the four cranes, those numbered 29-31 are capable of lifting three tons each, whilst the fourth, number 32 can manage a whopping 10 tons. During the 1950s, eight of these cranes could be found along Princes Wharf and there were over 40 dotted about the harbour. The cranes' massive heights meant they could easily retrieve goods from even very large vessels which could then be placed on waiting trains that would dispatch them to Temple Meads and around the country.

They were last put to work in the role of international trade in 1974, when they were used to lift wood from the Baltic from a ship - Baltic wood had long been prized by shipwrights for its sturdiness and relative affordability.

When the harbour stopped operating as a commercial port in 1975, there were not only concerns about what would become of the docks but how private companies who had owned the cranes could financially support themselves, so plans were soon afoot to sell off the cranes around the harbour for scrap metal.

There was outrage across the city. It was one thing for Bristol to lose the prestige of international importance but quite another to see the last remnants of its heritage ripped away.

A campaign group named City Docks Ventures - a member of which was George Ferguson, the man who would become Bristol's first ever elected mayor - aimed to save four of these electric cranes from the scrapyard and set about raising funds. Eventually they had enough to purchase two of them and in the words of City Docks Ventures themselves, "shamed" the council for not having done more to preserve the legacy of Bristol's docks.

The council finally submitted to rising pressure by agreeing to buy two more of the cranes and eventually bought the two which belonged to City Docks Ventures, ensuring that they would go on to loom high over the city.

For many years they remained immobile and unused, but in 2001 a small band of volunteers began working on restoring the cranes into working order and thanks to their efforts, all four cranes are now in pristine condition - and are an impressive sight to behold in action. Not only do they give semi-regular "rides" to visitors, but are also used to stock and rearrange the collections held at both M-Shed and L-Shed.

The existence of the four cranes along Princes Wharf are a triumph of determination. Without the enthusiasm and conviction of people who saw the importance of these cranes, Bristol would have lost not just icons of its harbourside, but important reminders of our city's past.

The next stop is the M-Shed. If it is open, I highly recommend travelling to the top floor balcony for easily one of the best views of the harbour you are ever likely to find.

2. M-Shed and the SS Great Western

Since opening in 2011, M-Shed, the museum celebrating (and commemorating) the history, people and places of Bristol has become a much loved fixture on the harbourside. Among its vast collection of artefacts, my personal highlights are the 14th century door to Spicer's Hall, the book of trial notes bound in the skin of murderer John Horwood, the Bristol Lodekka bus, the death mask of Alfred the Gorilla and the permanent exhibition detailing Bristol's historic involvement with the slave trade.

M-Shed and its adjoining warehouse, L-Shed were built in the 1950s to replace a large granary which had been destroyed during the Bristol Blitz. Warehouses around the harbour were often alphabetised to distinguish them from one another, which is why the M-Shed is so named - and also why a bar across the water is called the V-Shed.

This location has been important to the city's history long before M-Shed was built. Running the length of where the warehouses now stand and extending into Wapping Wharf, there was once a huge dry dock, used for shipbuilding. Far and away the most significant ship ever constructed here was Isambard Kingdom Brunel's paddle steamer, the SS Great Western.

Measuring 71.6 metres in length, when the Great Western was launched 1837 she was the largest passenger ship ever built. Weighing a staggering 1,340 tons, it had been theorised by many that the oak-hulled leviathan was simply too big and heavy to float. These fears were allayed when the paddle steamer made a graceful departure from the city to a stunned audience of onlookers who had never seen a vessel so huge. After successfully navigating her way through the serpentine River Avon, the SS Great Western set sail to London where she was fitted with a pair of steam engines.

Her maiden voyage from Bristol to New York was something of a public relations disaster initially, as a fire onboard as the ship reached the Avonmouth Docks spooked so many of the passengers that fifty of them immediately cancelled their tickets and departed the ship, leaving only seven behind for the maiden transatlantic crossing.

This catastrophic piece of publicity was soon forgotten when the SS Great Western docked in New York just 21 days after leaving Bristol. This was an astonishing feat for the time and with an average speed of almost 9 knots, Brunel's ship obliterated the previous speed record for an Atlantic crossing.

The ship remained in service between Bristol and New York for eight years until her operator, the Great Western Steamship Company collapsed, following contractual complications, whereupon she was put into service as a mail and goods transporter. Later still, she was repurposed to deliver British soldiers to fight in the Crimean War before finally being scrapped in 1856.

The next stop on our journey is on the harbour just outside M-Shed. The Mayflower is a medium sized boat which can usually be found moored along Princes Wharf when it is not in operation.

3. Mayflower

The tugboat Mayflower may at first look like an insubstantial vessel when compared to some of the larger ships which have found a permanent home in Bristol's harbour, but if you've ever seen her out of the water on the Patent slipway at Underfall Yard, you will appreciate that she is a deceptively large vessel with a very deep hull.

Mayflower can boast some remarkable claims to fame, the most notable is possibly that she is the oldest ship still afloat in the harbour. Built in 1861, the SS Great Britain may predate her by twenty years, but Brunel's masterpiece is permanently stationed in the dry dock in which she was built.

Mayflower is also believed to be the oldest Bristol-built ship that is still in operation anywhere in the world. She was constructed as part of a fleet of similar steam tugs by G. K. Stothert & Co., a subsidiary of the Bath-based Stothert & Pitt, who built most of the surviving cranes which can still be found around the harbour.

Finally, Mayflower is the oldest surviving tugboat in the world. Tugboats were built to guide larger ships into narrow harbours and waterways. Before their invention, the delicate operation was performed by horses, who would pull ships from bridleways along the edges of well-used shipping routes.

For many years, it was believed that it would be impossible for any small vessel to ever rival horsepower and dockers working at Sharpness Canal, where the Mayflower spent most of her working life, had to be persuaded with demonstrations where a tug would essentially "race" a horse while both tugged a boat.

The demonstrations proved successful and soon canals from Sharpness to Gloucester were being serviced by G.K. Stothert & Co's speedy, efficient tugboats.

Mayflower has undergone many adaptations throughout her long career. Perhaps the most remarkable was the hinging of her funnel so that she was able to pass under low bridges and tunnels - making her invaluable in navigating smaller waterways around Bristol.

By 1967, it seemed as if Mayflower's distinguished career had come to its natural end and her owners, British Waterways, sold her for scrap. However, as is so often the case with these historic relics, her salvation came in the form of a band of plucky enthusiasts, in this case a group of friends led by 20 year old Barrett Wyrley, who successfully won the auction for Mayflower thanks to a loan from his cousin.

Over the course of six years, Mayflower was gradually restored to working order and was once again put up for auction - this time to be preserved as part of Bristol maritime heritage. She was bought by Bristol Museums & Art Gallery and has spent her retirement in the harbour (and occasionally the River Avon) providing fun and informative trips to visitors and locals alike.

Just next door to the Mayflower can be found two other boats, often tethered to each other. One is a tug boat named John King and the other is Pyronaut.

4. John King and Pyronaut

One of the best aspects of summer in Bristol is getting to see our historic ships in action. The Harbourside Festival will have the full set in operation throughout the weekend, but sometimes just walking along the harbour you may be met with the glorious surprise of a handsome old boat touring through the waterway.

The John King and Pyronaut were built just a year apart but could not be more different in purpose. Of the two, the John King is the slightly younger, having been built in 1935.

Her name comes from John King, the founder of a small shipbuilding company named CJ King Tugs Ltd, which had funded the construction of many similar tugboats. The company had a respectably sized fleet of tug boats which operated in and around Bristol, with her main function being to escort ships up and down the perilous River Avon.

In 1970, the John King was tasked with her most famous and important assignment, when she was chosen to be one of the vessels which would bring what was left of the SS Great Britain into the dry dock where she has stood ever since. The John King would be the boat which led the way through the Avon, with the SS Great Britain towed behind her.

It was a nerve-racking time for all involved, as no one was sure if the mighty ship would be capable of floating on her own once she had been freed from the pontoon which had carried her across the Atlantic, but she floated - and the John King performed her precise passage to the city with perfection.

The Pyronaut was built exclusively to serve the Bristol docks. Launched in 1934, she was known as a "fire-float", a kind of firefighting vessel which patrolled the harbour.

She was built to sit low enough in the water that she could speedily pass under all of Bristol's Bridges without need to wait for them to lift or swing. For many decades she was moored at Phoenix Wharf, close to the entrance to the Redcliffe Caves where a small building, which can still be found, served as the fire station for her crew. The building now serves as a temporary art exhibition space but a plaque on its exterior celebrates its former purpose.

Pyronaut's abilities were tested to their limit during WWII, when the small ship was present at every bombing around the harbour. The most significant of these was on the night of the 24th of November when an enormous blitz destroyed almost all of the heavily populated area of the city which is now Castle Park.

The majority of the arsenal which rained onto the area were incendiary bombs, designed to spread fires quickly through the mostly wooden houses. Pyronaut was one of the first emergency vehicles at the scene and was able to reach parts of the inferno which were inaccessible from anywhere else, thanks to massive pumps capable of spraying 40 litres of water per second.

Pyronaut was probably responsible for saving many lives that night, and countless more throughout her years of active service until she was sold in 1973 and repurposed as a diver's boat.

She was bought by Bristol City Museum and Art Gallery in 1989 and converted back to a fire-float, only this time to perform demonstrations and displays of her impressive pumps around the harbour. In 1995, she and the John King were moored outside what is now M-

Shed, and the two sisters have had a home there ever since.

The next stop is for the Matthew. Another ship, but this time a wooden one. Head west along the harbour to the edge of M-Shed where you will find the handsome, triple masted ship.

5. The Matthew

When John Cabot set sail from Bristol to the New World in 1497, it's unlikely that he could have had any inkling of just how fondly the city would come to remember him. More than 500 years since his daring voyage across the Atlantic, he is regarded as one of the most significant people in the history of Bristol - quite an achievement for a man from Genoa, Italy who only spent a little time in the city!

The commemoration of Cabot and his achievements is nothing new. In 1897, to mark the 400th anniversary of the crossing, Cabot Tower on Brandon Hill was constructed - a beautiful icon of the city's skyline which also celebrates the kinship between Britain and America. For the 5th centenary of Cabot's voyage, the replica ship The Matthew was built.

Calling it a replica of the Matthew is not specifically true, and the trust which owns the ship is at pains to explain how very little is known of what Cabot's ship actually looked like, aside from that it was able to house no more than twenty men.

The new Matthew was built to a design by naval architect Colin Mundie, whose extensive research concluded the vessel was most likely a caravel - a type of small ship capable of making long journeys and favoured by Mediterranean countries. Mundie, along with a team of twelve shipwrights set about constructing the Matthew ahead of the 1997 anniversary and it was completed in 1996.

At the ship's launch, the Matthew was christened not with the traditional bottle of champagne but with a bottle of Bristol Cream sherry. After some tests of seaworthiness were performed in the English Channel, the Matthew was deemed capable of retracing the path across the Atlantic Cabot had made many centuries before.

On the night before she left Bristol, Cabot Tower repeatedly blinked "GOD SPEED MATTHEW" in morse code and on the morning of the 2nd of May, 1997, the harbour was lined with thousands of onlookers who waved the ship and her small crew away on their journey - exactly five hundred years to the day since Cabot's voyage.

The crossing was a rough one for even hardened seafarers, with the round-bottomed boat bobbing about like a barrel on the vast ocean. Nevertheless, she made it to Canada on schedule and on the afternoon of the 24th of June, the Matthew sailed into Bonavista, Newfoundland, where she was met by Queen Elizabeth II.

Even relying on modern radio capabilities, the crossing of the Atlantic by the new Matthew was a daring triumph and one which reminded the people of Bristol just what an important role their city had once played in shaping the history of the world.

The next stop on our walk is the Fairbairn Crane. Continue west along the harbour for a little bit until you see the battleship-grey structure with a bent crane arm overhead.

6. The Fairbairn Crane

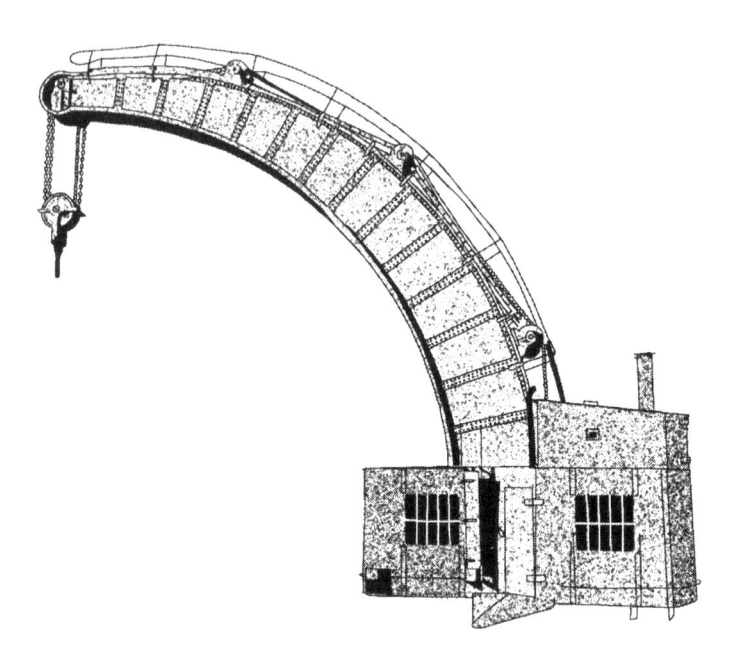

The Fairbairn steam crane is easily the most unusual crane to be found in Bristol today. Its curved arm and squat control room set it apart from the elegant, upright contraptions, but its uniqueness is not confined to Bristol alone - there is no other crane like this left in the world.

Fairbairn cranes were designed and patented by Scottish engineer Sir William Fairbairn, 1st baronet of Ardwick in 1850. Fairbairn had an enviable array of patents to his name, mostly involving steelwork and shipbuilding. By the time the Bristol Fairbairn crane was erected, in 1878, he had been dead for four years, but had lived to see his design implemented in ports across the world.

The Fairbairn crane was built to accommodate the increase of water traffic into Bristol Harbour. Since 1809, when the Floating Harbour was constructed, Bristol had become increasingly important to international trade and in order to keep up with competition from ports such as Liverpool, it became necessary to build a crane capable of raising much heavier loads.

Not only did the Fairbairn crane allow the docks to process much larger cargo weights, it obliterated the previous five ton limit to an astonishing 35 tons. The almighty power of the crane may be hard to fathom, but that's about equal to raising over 50 concert-sized grand pianos in a single lift.

The Fairbairn crane also had the benefit of being built next to the newly constructed harbourside railways, meaning that enormous cargos could be brought from the holds of ships and placed onto trains in a matter of minutes. It was a revolutionary design for Bristol and one which increased the city's stature and importance even further.

The formidable power of the Fairbairn crane is all the more impressive when you consider that, despite being the oldest surviving crane in the harbour, its weight limit is almost twice that of all other Bristol cranes combined.

Fairbairn's design proved to be very popular, but Bristol seems to have been the only place in the world to truly appreciate the innovation of the crane, as all other steam-powered Fairbairn cranes on the planet have been scrapped - and though a few hand-cranked versions are still in existence, Bristol is the only place on earth where this remarkable feat of steam engineering not only still stands - but is in fully working order.

Continue westward to the entrance of the SS Great Britain. It is simply impossible to overrate this historic marvel, it is one of Bristol's truly world-class attractions and something everyone should experience. If you have the time and money, I of course recommend a break from this walk to explore the ship and museums, but if you are stretched for either, you can just about catch a glimpse of this beautiful piece of engineering from the entrance.

7. The SS Great Britain Mystery

There are so many wonders to be found around the harbourside but it's hard to deny that the true jewel in the crown is the multi-award winning SS Great Britain ship and museum. Almost everybody is aware of the basic facts of this remarkable ship - it was a groundbreaking achievement by Isambard Kingdom Brunel, it was scuttled at sea but re-floated thanks to a gargantuan effort and returned to Bristol in 1970 as little more than a ghost of its former self and later converted into the city's most popular visitor attraction, but few are aware that the ship is home to a sad and haunting mystery which will likely never be sold.

John Gray was born in 1819 on the island of Unst - the northernmost inhabited place in the British Isles. From a young age he showed an interest in seafaring and began working on, and later being the master mariner of many ships.

By 1852 he was offered the position of Second Mate on the SS Great Britain, and although this position would have paid less than his work for the merchant navy, he accepted the role, becoming captain of the ship just two years later.

Gray was captain when her outward destination changed from New York to Melbourne and in total, he made 27 trips to and from Australia over his 18 years in charge of the vessel.

He was said to have been an imposing figure - huge in stature and presence and a formidable opponent to members of his crew who had misbehaved onboard, yet diplomatic in his approach to passengers' complaints.

Despite his austere nature, he was highly regarded as a fair yet stern captain with a tremendous affection for the ship, which he said he often patted and congratulated when she had performed particularly well, however, unbeknownst to none but a handful of confidantes, Gray suffered from several maladies, including stomach and liver troubles, which he believed were due to his constant anxieties about maintaining the ship's reputation as one of the finest vessels in the world.

On the night of the 25th of November, 1872, the SS Great Britain was returning from Melbourne and was about halfway through its journey. Gray had complained about stomach pains earlier that evening and was later witnessed writing a letter in his cabin. Close to midnight he was seen taking the stairs from his cabin to the deck. This would be the last time anybody saw Captain John Gray again.

The following morning, a ship's steward brought the captain his breakfast and found his bed empty and untouched. An immediate search of the ship was made but no sign of the man could be found. Later, a window was found to have been opened on the lower deck saloon but this was the only detail that seemed to be different from any other morning aboard the SS Great Britain.

Tragically, word could not get out to Liverpool before the ship's arrival into dock in January and Gray's wife and daughter, who had come to greet him, had to be informed of his mysterious disappearance and presumed death.

Theories as to what happened to the captain range from suicide (although this presumption rests on the idea that the letter he was seen writing that evening was a suicide note - despite no trace of that letter ever being found), to an accident or even murder.

Although it's said that the ghost of Captain John Gray has on occasion been sighted in the dining saloon of the ship he had such great affection for, it is almost certain that the strange, sad mystery of his disappearance will never be solved.

Our next stop is right where you are. We are going to examine the near miracle which brought the SS Great Britain home to Bristol all those years ago.

8. Bringing the Grand Old Lady Home

It's hard to imagine the harbour without the SS Great Britain, but it may be harder still to imagine that this beautiful triumph of industrial age engineering was once left neglected and rotting on a seabed halfway around the world.

The Facts of the ship remain staggering. The SS Great Britain was a marvel of her age. Designed by Brunel and the first iron hulled transatlantic ship, it was powered by steam which drove an enormous screw propeller, capable of driving the almighty ship from Bristol to New York in less than a fortnight.

However, as revolutionary as she was, the SS Great Britain was at the mercy of the changing fortunes of the Victorian era and was refitted and repurposed several times over her long and distinguished working life. Once she was overtaken by bigger and faster ships along the transatlantic route, she was sent to Australia, where she took immigrants (often over 700 with every voyage) hoping to exploit the newly discovered gold fields in Victoria.

She served this purpose until 1881 when she was fitted out to work as a coal transporter. One year later, a fire spread throughout the ship and she was left stranded on a sand bank in the Falklands Isles.

Over many years she was occasionally picked apart for metal or valuables but mostly remained untouched, save for the ravages of time and the sea. By 1937 she was in such a sorry condition that she was towed out to deeper waters, scuttled and forced to sink to the seabed, with only her upper deck and masts visible above the water. It was here she would rest - and rot for more than thirty years.

In 1969, naval architect Ewan Corlett began concocting an audacious plan. What if it was possible to salvage the SS Great Britain and bring the ship once known as "The Grand Old Lady" all the way back to her birthplace of Bristol?

Corlett knew he would need money, so he approached private investors, among them was Sir Jack Arnold, a businessman who was also president of the Wolverhampton Wanderers football club and philanthropist John Paul Getty Jr. of the famous (and infamous) Getty family.

In April of 1970, work began on patching up holes and cracks in the hull, with welders hastily bolting much of the ship back together. Trenches were dug into the sea bed and the almighty vessel was gently moved onto a pontoon which was then raised to sea level.

For 8,000 miles the SS Great Britain was towed across the Atlantic in what would be her final voyage. While out on the ocean she weathered storms and rough seas for two months before she arrived in Avonmouth to an enormous fanfare.

At the docks she received an inspection and repairs to some of her water damage before undertaking the last part of her journey - one which would require her to float unassisted.

Flanked by tugboats on all sides, she was gently removed from the pontoon and then, for the first time in almost 90 years, the SS Great Britain was completely buoyant.

For the final leg of her journey, the Grand Old Lady was greeted by up to 100,000 people, cheering her arrival from both sides of the River Avon. Despite looking like a skeleton of her former self, the jubilation was enormous. She was Bristol's ship and she had come home.

She waited at the lock junction for a further two weeks until the tide conditions were just right but on the 19th of July (127 years to the day since she had been launched) she was towed into the Floating Harbour and then slid into place in the Great Western Dry Dock where she had once been built.

The squeeze was so tight it knocked off many of the mussels which had clung to the ship's hull. Later that evening these were cooked and served as part of a celebration for her safe journey back to Bristol.

Turn left onto Gas Ferry Road. About half way along there is a small path on the right which takes you to Bristol Marina and Hanover Place. There is a cream coloured building with a clock tower on the edge of a car park and on a section of wall facing the harbour is an enigmatic mural of a woman's face.

9. Banksy

The legacy of the world-renowned street artist known as Banksy can be seen all across Bristol, with many of his best loved pieces found scattered across the city. The mural on the edge of a car park in Hanover Place, however, is one of his least visited creations in Bristol.

Appearing overnight in October, 2014 and called *Girl with a Pierced Eardrum*, Banksy subverts Johannes Vermeer's *Girl with a Pearl Earring* by substituting the building's burglar alarm for the piece of jewellery.

Although the artist chooses to remain anonymous - owing to his years of having to evade the police as a street artist, speculation is rife online as to who his identity may be, with many names recurring, sometimes with supposedly corroborating evidence to support the suspect. There is also a theory that Banksy may no longer be one person and that his mastery of multiple forms of media suggests that "Banksy" may now refer to more of a collective than any single person.

What little details can be said with some confidence are that Banksy was born in Bristol in the early 1970s and took to street art in his teen years. The 1990s were an interesting time for the city, with an underground music scene merging with street art to create a kind of counterculture movement epitomised by what was known as the Bristol Sound. It's thought that it was here that Banksy forged his craft and identity.

Many of his early Bristol works have been lost, either through neglect, accident or intentional removal and a few others have been vandalised (including the Girl with a Pierced Eardrum, but the black paint splatters mostly hit a dark area of the mural so it wasn't noticeably damaged.)

In 2009, Bristol Museum and Art Gallery hosted Banksy vs Bristol Museum - an exhibition of over 100 pieces of work from the artist which was installed in the museum by Banksy and kept secret to all but a few museum curators until the day before the exhibition opened.

Banksy vs Bristol Museum was an unprecedented success which further established the artist's ties to the city. Over 12 weeks it attracted more than 300,000 visitors - making it one of the most visited art exhibitions by a living artist in history.

For the final stop on this walk, we are heading back to the water. On the west side of the marina there is a slipway heading down into the harbour. This is where we're going next.

10. The Harbour's Unexpected Visitor

From the slipway beside Bristol Marina, it is sometimes possible to see a preponderance of fish in the water on especially fine days and this spot has also proven popular with a great deal of waterfowl. The shape of the harbour seems to funnel aquatic weeds into this spot, making it a perfect place to spend some time appreciating the often overlooked wildlife which has found a home in Bristol. It was also the spot where, in 2005, a rather unexpected visitor was witnessed.

There seems to be a general, but unfair assumption among many Bristolians that the harbour water is dirty, diseased and dangerous. Although it's probably not advisable to drink any of it, the Floating Harbour is considered to be of better quality than can be found in most cities of equivalent size - and the array of wildlife that can be found within it is testament to the improved cleanliness of our waterways.

Since the docks ceased to operate as a commercial harbour, the water quality has improved steadily. The better water has meant an increase in fish, which in turn has attracted some of Bristol's favourite feathered residents - the handsome cormorants who patrol the harbour (and occasionally the sea lion enclosure at Bristol Zoo) in search of fish. Just as common are swans, ducks and geese. In recent years otters have been spotted near Castle Park and a small family seem to have made the harbour its home, but in 2005 a truly remarkable visitor came to Bristol.

Early reports of a seal being witnessed in the River Avon and the Floating Harbour were initially shrugged off as preposterous but when a photograph was snapped of what was unmistakably a seal close to the Feeder Canal, the proof was undeniable.

Owing to the photograph being taken near to Whitby Road, the creature was soon dubbed "Whitby" and briefly became a seldom seen but much sought after local celebrity. The slipway at Bristol Marina was claimed to be the location of one of the final sightings of the enigmatic beast when it was seen diving for fish. Soon afterwards he or she vanished from Bristol altogether.

A short while afterwards, a dead seal was found washed up in Portishead and though there were fears that this was Whitby, seals are far more common towards the Severn than Bristol, so it's quite possible it was an unrelated creature.

Whatever the truth, there's no harm in hoping that Whitby enjoyed his or her brief visit to Bristol before safely returning to the sea.

That concludes our casual stroll around the harbour. From here I recommend The Cottage Inn for a pint or a snack at Underfall Yard's Pickle Cafe. From there you can go on to start another walk, which takes you beyond the edge of the harbour and begins on page 193.

Walk Four
Central Bristol

Central Bristol

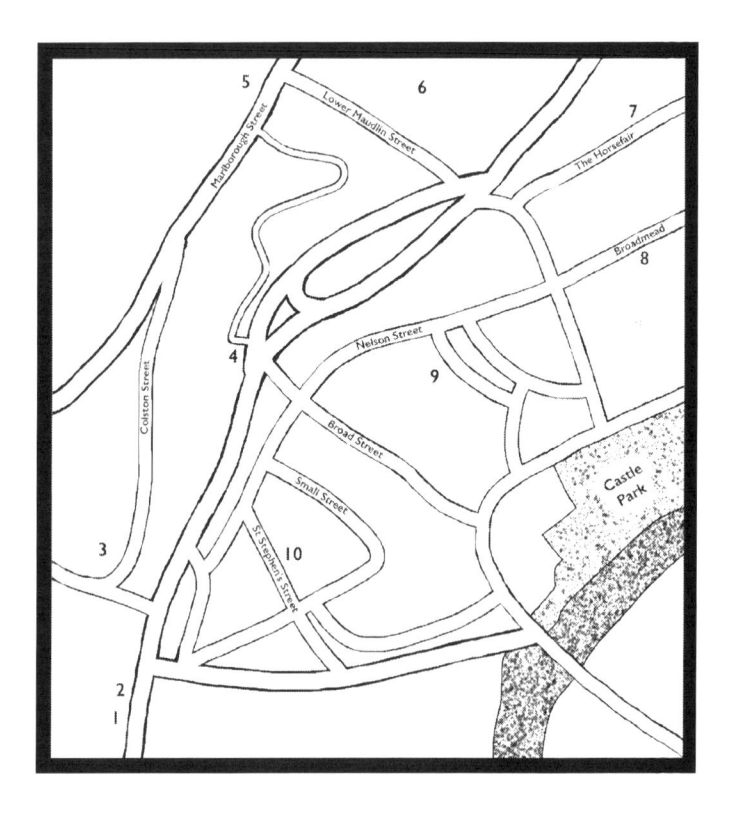

Whenever something significant happened in the history of Bristol, there's a good chance it happened right in the heart of the city.

This walk will take you through almost a thousand years of history, from the time Bristol was a small town on the edge of a river to one of the largest cities in the country.

Along the way we will have encounters with a trans pioneer who abandoned the aristocracy to become a

Buddhist monk, an ambitious but failed attempt to build a "city in the sky" and a chaotic night at Colston Hall with the biggest band in the history of the world…

This walk begins outside the Hippodrome.

1. The Hippodrome Fire

The Hippodrome opened on the 16th of December 1912. On its opening night it staged a blockbuster extravaganza called "The Sands O' Dee", a variety show which utilised the theatre's most unusual feature, a tank built into the stage which was filled with 450,000 litres of water. The pool hosted not only elaborate dance numbers but horses high-diving from raised platforms. The crowds were ecstatic and had never seen a spectacle like it before - few people had - as at the time no theatre in the country was larger - save for the London Coliseum.

Like the Coliseum, the Hippodrome was designed by architect Frank Matcham, who specialised in building theatres. Matcham honoured the city's maritime history by incorporating details such as porthole windows and mosaics depicting naval achievements. The interior was inspired by opulent liners of the age such as Titanic and Mauretania, with sweeping staircases and wood-lined walls. Bristol had never experienced a night out like this before.

The theatre hosted mainly variety shows and reviews until 1932, when it was converted into a cinema for a few years. The cinema was initially popular but because of competition from cheaper venues in the city, it reverted back to staging theatrical productions in 1938.

Despite the dwindling popularity of variety shows the Hippodrome continued staging them and it was not until November 1940, when the nearby Prince's Theatre on Park Row was destroyed by a German bomb, that it began to feature more narrative-led productions.

Aside from some light shrapnel damage, the Hippodrome survived largely unscathed through WWII, but on the afternoon of the 19th of February 1948 a huge fire devastated the theatre.

It's believed that the fire either started beneath the stage or behind it. At the time it was suggested that it could have been caused by a discarded cigarette but no definite cause was ever found.

Throughout history, fires in theatres have proven to be among the most costly to human life. The most notorious was the Chicago Iroquois Theatre fire of 1903, where most of the over 600 deaths were due to the stampede of people and the fact that the exit doors could not be opened as they swung inwards where a massive crush of people were fighting to escape. For this reason, the Hippodrome and all British theatres were built with fire doors which opened outwards.

No such emergency exits were required that day as the auditorium was empty but there were a dozen or so stagehands in the building. Despite the fire spreading quickly, there was very little panic in the Hippodrome and the staff calmly but quickly left the building.

The emergency services were quick to respond and fire engines were soon on the scene, as was the fire-float Pyronaut, which hosed down the Hippodrome from the harbour. Some of the men leaving the theatre reported being drenched as they escaped the fire, thanks to the Pyronaut's incredible water pressure being sprayed into the foyer, but there were no reported injuries.

The fire was extinguished within an hour but the theatre was in a sorry state. The stage was completely destroyed and part of the ceiling had collapsed. Backstage, there was almost nothing left which hadn't been turned to ash.

It wasn't just the speedy efforts of the emergency services that saved the Hippodrome but the mammoth operation the theatre put into action to rebuild the much-loved theatre. Astonishingly, the theatre opened its doors again on Christmas Eve of 1948, looking immaculate for that year's pantomime - Cinderella.

Next to the Hippodrome is a pub called the Drawbridge. Over the entrance there is a figure of a man holding a spear. He will be the focus of our next stop.

2. The Demerara Figure

On the outside of the Drawbridge pub - the popular venue beside the Hippodrome - there is a rather curious figure of a man. He has stood guard over St Augustine's Parade for decades but few people know the full story of his origins.

In his left hand he holds a spear, while in his right he holds what is thought to be tobacco leaves. The man represents a Native American and it has been suggested that the pose, proffering goods while bearing a weapon, may symbolise the uneasy relationship merchants had with the native people they encountered.

The statue is inspired by what was once one of the most familiar sculptures in the city. The original was about twice the height of the man outside the Drawbridge and was made as a ship's figurehead rather than a traditional statue.

One of the earliest photographs of a Bristol street was taken in the 1850s of Small Street (now Colston Street) and depicts the Demerara figure outside a tobacconists.

The statue is so named because it was built as the figurehead on the front of the steamship SS Demerara, which was built in Bristol. The Demerara was the second largest ship ever built (after the SS Great Britain) and was wrecked on her maiden voyage when she hit a sandbank in the River Avon in 1851. The vessel had to be salvaged and rebuilt as a smaller ferry ship and sometime during this operation her figurehead went missing, only to resurface on Small Street.

The Demerara figure was a much-loved fixture of Small Street for decades, but the elements took their toll and in the 1930s an attempt to remove him from the building for renovations resulted in him crumbling away into little more than dust.

The sad demise of the Demerara figure resulted in a replica being commissioned, which eventually was given pride of place on the Drawbridge Pub, overlooking the Centre. What little remains of the original can now be found in M-Shed.

Continue along the Centre with your back to St Augustine's Reach. A road bends to the left and up a slight hill towards Colston Hall.

3. The Beatles at Colston Hall

At the time of writing the Colston Hall is still operating under that name but is due to rename itself sometime in 2020.

The Colston Hall opened in 1867 and was built to a Bristol Byzantine style which has been greatly expanded upon over the intervening century and a half, most notably with the 2009 extension which features a stunning, multi-storeyed foyer.

As a music venue, Colston Hall has attracted some of the most distinguished and popular musical acts from around the world, including Johnny Cash, Bob Dylan, Queen and David Bowie. During the 1960s the venue had successfully shaken off its reputation for being somewhat out of touch by attracting a series of high-profile bookings - among them were the Beatles, who performed at the Colston Hall on two legendary nights.

Their first appearance was on the 15th of March 1963 when the band performed a set of ten songs to a euphoric crowd. Outside the venue there were scenes of near riot, with fans attempting to break through a security cordon to get a glimpse of the musicians.

In the days following the performance there were calls in the local press to ban the Beatles from ever appearing in Bristol again, for fear of them causing the youth of Bristol to run amuck. At the time, many of these complaints were dismissed as having come from embittered journalists who had been unable to secure tickets to the show.

Nevertheless, the Beatles did return to Bristol and took to the Colston Hall stage on Tuesday the 10th of November 1964.

The penultimate song of the set was *If I fell* from the band's album *Hard Day's Night*. During the closing section, students who had managed to break into the lighting gantry above the stage poured flour on the heads of the Fab Four.

The prank was taken in good humour by the Beatles who finished up their set as planned. Later that evening, it was said that Paul McCartney met his then-girlfriend Jane Asher (who was performing in a production of St Trinians at the Old Vic) at the Gryphon Pub on Colston Street, a fanciful yet possibly true version of the story has Asher still in her schoolgirl costume and McCartney still covered in flour.

One person who did not take kindly to the stunt was theatre manager Ken Howley, who was furious not just at the mess that had been made but concerned that the Beatles would not want to perform at his venue again.

The Beatles never did perform at the Colston Hall again, but not because of the flour prank. Following a disastrous 1966 world tour where the band were plagued by sound issues (often not being able to hear themselves over the screams of the crowd) and also fears that Beatlemania had got so out of control their safety was at risk, the band decided that live performances had become too much of a burden and the Fab Four never toured again.

Return to St Augustine's Parade and head north past the bottom of Christmas Steps and towards Hotel Du Vin, besides which there is an entranceway to a narrow passage with the signage "Johnny Ball Lane". This is the location of our next stop.

4. Johnny Ball Lane

Tucked away out of sight behind Lewin's Mead and unknown to many Bristolians is Johnny Ball Lane - one of the strangest little passages in the city.

Walking up the lane can be an intimidating experience. It is narrow and has high walls on either size, rendering it gloomy on even the sunniest days. At the halfway point there is, for me at least, that slight feeling of apprehension upon realising how closed in the passageway feels - there is no means of escape and for centuries this was exploited by some of the most violent criminals in Bristol's history.

Most people who have heard of Johnny Ball Lane know it for its peculiar name. The temptation to imagine it was named after the popular mathematician and children's TV presenter (who was born in Bristol) is hard to resist, but the name is thought to originate from a local man named John a Ball who owned property beside a nearby friary in the 15th century.

In the 18th century a plot of land near to the lane was reserved for the Bristol Royal Infirmary. The practice during this time was that people who had succumbed to disease should be buried as quickly as possible, so it's unknown how many people may have been interred under what is now a labyrinth of busy streets.

It was also at this time that the lane became notorious for violent muggings. It's said that during the Georgian era doctors and surgeons would brandish swords and even surgical tools when going to and from the Infirmary after dark. Sometimes even these measures were not enough to fend off the determined robbers, who would think nothing of leaving a man for dead after stealing all his valuable possessions.

Nowadays it's a curious oddity in the heart of the city which offers a unique - though somewhat chilling - experience for those daring enough to brave it.

If you decided to brave the lane it will guide you to Marlborough Street. Once there, turn right and head down the hill until you see a large, grey building on the other side of the road which is far older than those around it. This is the Bristol Royal Infirmary Old Building.

The lane is very narrow, so if you're claustrophobic or get anxious in tight spaces, continue along Lewin's Mead and take a left at the junction onto Lower Maudlin Street which will lead you past the White Hart pub and to the Royal Infirmary building at the top of the hill.

5. Michael Dillon: Trans Pioneer

The Bristol Royal Infirmary was established in 1735, making it one of the oldest hospitals in the country, but the building on Marlborough Street most commonly called the "Old Building" was added to the hospital a little later, being built between 1789 and 1814.

In the middle of the 20th century it played a small yet significant role in the extraordinary life of Michael Dillon.

Dillon was born in Folkestone, Kent in 1915 to Robert Arthur Dillon, heir to the baronetcy of Lismullen, Ireland, and named after his wife, Laura Maud McCliver. Assigned as female from birth and raised as such, Laura Dillon never felt comfortable in traditionally "girls'" clothing and took to wearing trousers from a young age.

As a young adult Dillon began self-identifying as a man, giving himself the name Laurence Michael Dillon, and was capable of passing as a man so easily that most people assumed he had been born biologically male.

During WWII, Dillon worked as a mechanic in a garage in Bristol. He had begun having testosterone injections which lowered his voice and allowed him to grow a beard. Most people in Dillon's life had now taken to referring to him as "he".

A couple of years after the end of the war, a chance encounter between Dillon and a plastic surgeon was to change his life entirely. Dillon was recuperating from a head injury in the Bristol Royal Infirmary when he met a cosmetic surgeon. Michael Dillon confided in him that he wished to use surgery to make himself appear more convincingly male and the surgeon was sympathetic.

While in Bristol, the surgeon performed a double mastectomy on Dillon before sending him to London to meet Harold Gillies, a surgeon who specialised in reconstructing soldier's genitals which had been severely wounded during the war.

Over the course of several years, Gillies performed a number of secret operations on Dillon and by 1949, Lawrence Michael Dillon finally believed he was in the body he was always meant to have. Though he did not know it at the time, he had been the first person in history to undergo female-to-male gender reassignment surgery.

Dillon's later years were no less eventful, including becoming both a physician and a distinguished rower. He also had a brief relationship with Roberta Cowell, the first British trans woman to receive male-to-female surgery.

Dillon prized his privacy above all things, so when a newspaper began investigating what had happened to Laura Dillion, the younger "sister" of who was by then the 8th Baronet of Lismullen and had seemingly vanished off the face of the earth, he began to panic and fled to India just as the full story was about to break.

In India, Michael joined a Buddhist community and eventually became the first European person to be ordained into the Rizong Monastery as a novice Buddhist monk. He remained part of the order until his visa expired in 1962. While making preparations to return to England he fell ill and was taken to a hospital in Dalhousie, India, where he subsequently died of an unknown illness, aged only 47.

Michael Dillon's extraordinary story is testament to one man's determination not to compromise his identity and though his life would take him halfway across the world, perhaps the most important step in his journey began right here in Bristol.

Follow Lower Maudlin Street downhill. Beside the White Hart pub there is an entrance to the grounds of St James' Priory - the subject of our next stop.

6. St James' Priory

Establishing what is truly the oldest building in Bristol is surprisingly contentious. Some of our oldest buildings were built far outside the city boundary, as part of adjacent towns and villages that Bristol eventually swelled to incorporate, while others have been torn apart and rebuilt so many times its unclear just how much of the original structure is still standing, but of all the buildings in Bristol, St James' Priory has the best claim to this prestigious title.

The original building dates back to 1129 when it was built as a priory. Bristol Cathedral may have a wall which is a little older than this, but the significant parts of the current structure weren't built until 1220.

In the almost 900 years since the priory was constructed Bristol has gone from little more than a small town on the edge of a river t0 one of the most populated cities in the country. However, much of St James' Priory could have been lost altogether were it not for a fortunate agreement made in 1374.

During the reign of Henry VIII, shortly after he had established the Church of England, a process known as the Dissolution of the Monasteries set about disbanding Catholic religious buildings such as priories and monasteries, stripping them of their valuables and often forcefully repurposing them for his own church. Sometimes the buildings were partly or even entirely demolished and it's believed that the nave of the priory would likely have succumbed to such a fate.

The nave of St James' Priory may only have been saved because in 1374 the Abbot of Tewksbury had decreed that the parishioners themselves would have authority over the building, meaning that when the church became the possession of the Crown in 1540, not even the authority of the king was enough to level what is now the oldest part of the building.

Nevertheless, the surrounding priory buildings were demolished and the building became significantly smaller - but the majority of it survived the dissolution.

St James' Priory survived not only Henry VIII, but was witness to one of the darkest chapters in Bristol history. When the plague hit the city it was said that bodies were piled high outside the church (as well as All Saints' Church on Corn Street). During WWII it emerged unscathed from the rubble, despite the obliteration of much of the surrounding area.

It even managed to survive that most formidable foe of Bristol's historic landmarks - 1960s town planners, who preserved the church's ground against expansion of the newly built Broadmead shopping centre.

It is now a Grade I listed building and one of our most important treasures.

Before leaving the grounds of St James' Priory, stop to see the lone remaining gravestone. This marks the resting place of several members of the Wesley family. The most significant member of this family was John Wesley, who founded Methodism and whose New Room was the first Methodist chapel in the world. It is where we shall be visiting next.

Follow the pathway downhill and cross the road. Then head left onto the Horsefair and follow it past the Arcade. On the right there is a statue of John Wesley marking the entrance to the New Room, it's worth having a look around if it's open.

Alternatively, you can begin a walk which explores the fascinating history of Picton Street. Follow the path which leads to the Bear

Pit and either go through or around it to Stokes Croft. Head north until you reach the junction with Ashley Road where the walk starts.

7. The New Room

Incongruously located in the middle of Bristol's largest shopping district, John Wesley's New Room is one of the most significant religious buildings in the city.

John Wesley was born in Lincolnshire in 1703 as the fifteenth of nineteen children (only nine of whom survived into adulthood.)

While at Oxford University, John and his older brother Charles founded an Anglican society and it was there that John first honed his skills as a priest and was ordained into the Church of England soon afterwards.

In his youth he toured the Province of Georgia - a British held colony of America now known simply as Georgia - and his experiences there led him to question some of the core doctrines he had been raised to believe, most importantly that of predestination - the concept that the course of a person's entire life is determined from birth by God's will.

After returning to Britain in 1737, Wesley converted to evangelism and began touring the country, particularly the south west of England, preaching what would become known as Wesleyan Theology - the belief that the path to salvation was through personal reflection and good deeds. He began preaching in support of both prison reform and charity towards the poor and also against slavery.

These meetings were usually held in the open air, a revolutionary concept stemming from the belief that the entire world is God's house, but attendance to these meetings was too dependent on the weather so Wesley began seeking a permanent venue from which his Wesleyan Theology (now known as Methodism) could be taught.

Bristol was chosen for two reasons. The land was affordable and the people of the city had taken to this new found interpretation of Anglicanism in impressive numbers. The New Room was completed in 1739 and was the first Methodist church built anywhere in the world.

Wesley wanted to keep the design of the New Room as minimalist as possible. He found the showy abundance of wealth a tasteless excess, so the design was kept basic and functional, making the most of the small space with two tiered seating and an elevated pulpit so preachers could be seen from both floors.

The pews themselves were recycled from ship's timber and to save money further a large octagonal window was installed in the ceiling, minimising the amount that would have to be paid in window tax and also allowing the space to be filled with an ethereal light as if from the heavens.

When not in religious use, the New Room also served as a school, teaching poor children (and sometimes adults too) how to read and write.

The New Room is a fascinating piece of Bristol history. I really do recommend a look around as it's a delightful, welcoming space and one which will continue to offer solace and reflection for many years to come.

Leaving via the second entrance to the New Room you will find yourself in a small courtyard which leads onto Broadmead. You should be facing a white fronted section of the Galleries Shopping Centre that looks out of place along the facade of shops. This will be our next destination.

8. The Greyhound Hotel

The white facade of a building that has seemingly been bolted onto the Galleries may look implausibly out of place, but this lesser-used entrance to the shopping centre is all that remains of the oldest hotel in Bristol - a building which predates everything in its surrounding area - including the New Room.

The facade itself is actually a precise replica, built in 1958 when the original was determined to be unstable, but the deep entranceway which passes through it is from the original hotel and was once used to guide horses and carts to a large courtyard beyond.

The Greyhound Hotel was built in 1620 and the courtyard served an important dual purpose. Not only could horses be securely stabled overnight but luggage could be hoisted up to individual rooms, saving weary travels the backbreaking labour of hauling their cases up flights of stairs.

The hotel was enormously popular. When it opened it was on a busy travelling route for coaches and was surrounded on all sides by open meadowland (Broadmead possibly derives its name from the "Broad Meadows" which surrounded the outskirts of the city. An alternate theory is that it comes from a type of woollen cloth called brodemedes which was woven in Bristol).

In 1775 a rival hotel was built next door to the Greyhound. Named the Bell, this new business could not compete with its neighbour and eventually was incorporated into the original hotel - making the Greyhound the largest coaching inn in Bristol.

During WWII the hotel narrowly avoided destruction during several raids on the city, but bombing completely obliterated Castle Street and Wine Street in the area around what is now Castle Park, which had been the city's busiest central shopping district. In the post war years it was clear that Bristol needed a radical overhaul which would include a dedicated shopping centre.

Work began in 1950 and shops were later installed in part of the Greyhound's lower floors, but the hotel, now mostly serving the role of a pub, continued operating until the early 1990s when the Galleries opened.

The expansion of Broadmead meant that Bristol lost one of its oldest establishments but in the entranceway to the remaining section of the old hotel there is a plaque commemorating the history and importance of the Greyhound, kept as a permanent reminder of our city's past.

If you pass through the entranceway into the Galleries, I recommend a quick detour by turning right and right again to the main entrance to the shopping centre. Just before leaving, have a look at the ground and you will see a bronze plaque on the floor. It was here that a time capsule containing items donated by pupils from Hartcliffe Secondary School was buried into the foundations of the building. The contents of the capsule have remained a secret.

After leaving the Galleries, head left past the Odeon Cinema and follow Nelson Street to the junction with All Saint's Street. Take a slight left until you see a ramp on the right heading into a rather gloomy looking complex of concrete mezzanines. This is our next stop on the walk.

9. The City in the Sky

Bristol's traffic problems are nothing new. For decades town planners have struggled to accommodate the city's expanding population and its increased reliance on roads.

The sheer number of waterways in the city have made this an onerous task. Bridges are expensive to construct and can damage picturesque views, so the traffic has had to contend with the ever present rivers in sometimes confusing ways, filtering through bottlenecks and long winded diversions.

Over the years many ideas have been put forward to alleviate the stress on our roads. One of the most radical came from the 1970s with a concept which would see large sections of our harbour filled in so roads could be built across it. Thankfully these plans never left the drawing board and our docks remained intact.

One plan which was instigated was dubbed the "City in the Sky" and the concrete section of walkways near St John on the Wall (separating it from its own churchyard) is the only part of Bristol where a section of this revolutionary but unpopular design can be found.

The idea was born of 1960s town planning and aimed to divide the city into two levels. At street level, the cars would dominate the roads while overhead elevated walkways made out of concrete would guide pedestrians about the city.

The plan was to have the entire city centre split in two, with cars and pedestrians almost never interacting. There were also plans for multi-level mezzanines with shops and restaurants.

It seemed like the perfect solution until the first sections of the design were built and it became apparent that the entire construction was gobsmackingly ugly. The walkways felt utilitarian and soulless. The mezzanines were gloomy and intimidating. On rainy days the entire complex was drenched a murky black and was prone to flooding.

The City in the Sky was abandoned shortly afterwards. Costs were skyrocketing and the complex was unpopular. Some sections of the design were still in place in what is now Cabot Circus but were among the first to be demolished when work began on the shopping centre in 2005.

As ugly and unfriendly the remaining section of the design may seem, it's still an interesting glimpse into what Bristol could have been.

Follow the City in the Sky as it runs parallel to Nelson Street. At Broad Street, go through the opening in the old city wall and head south along the Centre. Go left at St Stephen's Street and head towards the church, which will be the subject of our next stop.

10. St Stephen's Church and Bell-Ringers

St Stephen's is the magnificent, imposing church which has loomed high over the city since the ornate tower was built in 1473. The church once stood on the edge of the harbour and its distinct design worked its way into the background of many paintings of Bristol's docks throughout the centuries.

The church tower once held six enormous bells which pealed on the hour from dawn until St Nicholas Market's curfew at 9pm. Nowadays the tower is home to a whopping twelve bells - as well as one of the oldest bell-ringing societies in the country.

It's not known exactly how old the society is but it has been continuously active since at least 1574 when Elizabeth I's arrival into the city was heralded by the pealing of the bells, which is said to have greatly pleased the queen.

For centuries the bell-ringers of St Stephen's have adhered to a strict list of instructions on how to properly behave, each with its own fine for wayward rule-breakers. A penalty of tuppence was instigated against anyone who swore while in the church, whilst the fine for "scoffing" at another campanologist was set at three pence. The most severe penalty that a bell-ringer could face was to enter the belfry without previously having knelt at the altar. A fine of sixpence was levelled for the first offence and the punishment for a second was permanent expulsion from the society.

These rules still exist to this day but their implementation is not enforced as rigorously as they once were.

In 1885 the church's clergyman took on an assistant - a man named Ramsay McDonald - who soon afterwards established a guild to educate underprivileged boys and young men in the church.

McDonald would go on to co-found the Labour Party and in 1929 became the United Kingdom's first Labour Prime Minister.

That concludes this walk through central Bristol. If you took this tour as an alternative route on the Harbourside walk, that walk continues on Narrow Quay on page 43. If you want to start another tour, head towards the Marriot Hotel beside College Green by following Park Street uphill. The College Green walk begins on the following page.

Walk Five
College Green

College Green

It is certainly one of the most beautiful green spaces in Bristol, but don't let appearances fool you…

College Green has an ancient history and one which predates most of the city. On this pocket-sized and simple walk there will be tales of a ghostly monk who haunts the cathedral, a heartwarming friendship between two post-war cities and a cold blooded double murder that happened in broad daylight…

This walk begins outside the Bristol Marriott Royal Hotel beside College Green.

1. The College Green Murders

College Green enjoys a reputation as one of the most popular open spaces in Bristol and it's easy to see why. With its dramatic backdrop of the cathedral and City Hall, the park is a quiet oasis of calm in the heart of a bustling city.

It can be hard to imagine, but this peaceful green was the site of one of the most gruesome and brutal murders in Bristol's history.

The 27th of September 1764 had been a bright autumnal day. By the afternoon, in a house on the edge of College Green beside the now demolished St Augustine's the Less church, Mrs Frances Ruscombe and her maid Mary Sweet were busying themselves when an intruder let himself in through an unlocked door.

What happened next was an act of barbarism so horrific it sent shock waves through the city. Both Frances and Mary were murdered.

Frances had her throat slashed and was beaten to the head with such force that part of her skull caved in. Mary's throat had been severed so deeply that she had almost been decapitated. Her jaw had been broken and her head stabbed with a cleaver.

A considerable sum of £90 had been stolen from the house in the form of gold coins but the perpetrator of this atrocity had left no trace of himself.

It was not just the random brutality of this outrage that sent fear throughout the city but the audacity of the murderer having struck in the middle of the day, in broad daylight, and in a busy area of Bristol with countless potential witnesses.

Frances Ruscombe's husband was first suspected of the crime but he had been at work that afternoon. All leads ran cold until an intriguing incident in 1767.

Edward Higgins was a notorious highwayman, burglar and general scoundrel. He was caught robbing a house in Laugharne, south Wales and was sentenced to death by hanging.

Upon the gallows he handed his executioner a note which confessed to not just the crime he was to be executed for but a string of other offences, including the murders of Ruscombe and Sweet.

Higgins was hanged but incredibly survived this ordeal and began to revive in the middle of his own postmortem whereupon a physician's assistant bludgeoned him to death.

Some have argued that Higgins' confession was not reliable and that he may have been attempting to posthumously increase his notoriety, but most people both then and now agree that he was the most likely culprit - including some evidence which puts Higgins in the Bristol region at the time.

The chilling murders on College Green were so horrific that the house remained mostly unoccupied for several decades and stood as a stark reminder of the crimes until 1868 when an estate agent named Walter William Hughs decided to build a luxury hotel on the spot where the house stood. The house was subsequently demolished and a new hotel, now named the Bristol Marriott Royal, was built in its place.

From the Marriott, walk towards the cathedral. If it is open go through to the gardens at the back of this magnificent building, where you will find a bronze sculpture which is evocative of a huddled figure within a lopsided ring. If the cathedral is closed, the sculpture can be seen from a lane which runs down the east side of the garden

2. "Refugee"

Nestled in the shady tranquility of Bristol Cathedral's sumptuous garden is Naomi Blake's 1980 sculpture "Refugee".

It has been described as being both reminiscent of someone seeking shelter from a storm and an embryo in utero, it can be hard to imagine that something as tender and beautiful as this piece could have been made by someone who had been witness to the greatest atrocity of the 20th century.

Naomi Blake was born into a large Jewish family in the city of Mukačevo, Czechoslovakia (now part of Ukraine). At birth she was named Zisel Dum and was the youngest of ten children.

Throughout much of WWII the extended Dum family had been moved into a Jewish ghetto on the outskirts of Mukačevo and in 1944 they were boarded onto cattle trucks and sent to Auschwitz.

Naomi and her sister Malchi were separated from the rest of their family and sent to work in a munitions factory where the pair set about secretly sabotaging the weaponry they were forced to make so that it wouldn't function.

Thirty-two members of Naomi's family were sent to Auschwitz. Only eight of them would survive, the rest perishing in the gas chambers.

In January 1945, word reached the guards at Auschwitz that the Soviet army was on its way to liberate the camp and Naomi, Malchi and most of the surviving prisoners were sent on a death march over miles of hostile terrain to the town of Loslau in Poland where 60,000 of the prisoners were to be transported to other camps around Europe.

Many of the prisoners were too frail from their incarceration to survive the journey and either died of exhaustion or were executed by guards. Naomi and Malchi managed to flee the death march and a hail of bullets. The sisters made their way back to Mukačevo on foot and by hitching rides. Later that year they were reunited with two surviving sisters and a brother.

Following the UN decision to partition Palestine, Naomi and the remaining members of her family moved to Israel. In 1948 she was injured by shrapnel from a bullet and while recuperating in hospital began carving a piece of olive wood into the shape of a dog she had been gifted as a child. Soon after this she officially changed her name to Naomi.

Her creative talents were undeniable and she took to sculpting with a natural aptitude. In 1952 she married a German refugee named Asher Blake and the pair moved to London. Ten years later she exhibited her work at Salon de Paris to positive reviews which likened her sculptures to those of Henry Moore and Barbara Hepworth.

According to Blake, *Refugee* is her expression of hope for harmony between the world's races and religions and the need for compassion towards those fleeing conflict. It is one of over 50 of her works on public display around the country, almost all of which reflect her hope for peace and belief in the inherent goodness of humanity.

When asked how she could be optimistic about the human spirit when she had survived the greatest monstrosity the world has ever witnessed she replied:

"There is something positive in the human figure - there is a lot of good in people… with my past, if I were pessimistic, somehow, it wouldn't have been worthwhile surviving."

Naomi Blake died in 2018 at the age of 94.

At the west side of the cathedral there is a stone archway which connects to the Central Library. This will be our next stop on the walk.

3. The Great Gatehouse

Often mistaken for being an ornate extension to Bristol Central Library, the Great Gatehouse (also known as the Abbey Gatehouse) is actually one of the oldest surviving structures in the city.

The ground floor storey was constructed in 1170 and was once part of an enormous wall which encircled much of what is now College Green. Within this wall was St Augustine's Abbey which was built in 1140 and would later be massively extended into Bristol Cathedral as well as a few smaller buildings which served as accommodation for monks associated with the abbey. The entire complex was known as a monastic precinct.

The first floor and the adjoining tower were built sometime around 1500 and much of the ornamentation, including four of the figures found in the niches, was added to the arch's north side. The four figures represent chronicler John Newland, Bristol nobleman and financier Robert Fitzharding, King Henry II and Robert Elyot - the architect who designed the extension - curiously, he's holding a miniature model of the gatehouse tower itself.

Elyot can also be found on the south side of the arch, this time holding a model of the entire gatehouse along with another figure of John Newland. They are accompanied by the Abbot John Snow and architect Edmund Knowle. These four were added in 1914 to replace ones which had become too weathered with age.

In 1542, the abbey fell to the Dissolution of the Monasteries and most of the monastic precinct was demolished, however, the gatehouse seems to have been saved purely for its architectural beauty.

During the Victorian era, the gatehouse became the subject of debate with some arguing that the earliest parts of the structure could not possibly date back to the 12th century as they are simply in too good a condition, however, most archaeologists agreed that the gatehouse really was as ancient as had been claimed and not a replica made centuries later.

It may not be the only remnant of the old monastic precinct that can still be found on College Green. It is claimed that the cathedral is haunted by the ghost of a monk who is seen wearing grey robes (a peculiar detail as the monks of the abbey wore black habits.) The monk is said to walk from the entrance of the cathedral towards the library, where he passes through a bricked up doorway. For reasons that have never been understood, this ghost is almost only ever seen at 4pm.

Follow the curved walkway which runs parallel to the stretch of water in front of City Hall. About halfway along there are some bronze plaques set into the ground, one of which reads "Hannover, Germany. 1947". This will be the subject of our next stop.

4. Bristol's Longest Friendship

HANNOVER, GERMANY, 1947

Below the line of flag poles which run the length of City Hall there are seven bronze plaques laid into the ground. Each of these bears the coat of arms of a town or city which has been "twinned" with Bristol along with the year of the twinning. These are: Hannover, Germany (1947), Bordeaux, France (1947), Porto, Portugal (1984), Tbilisi, Georgia (1988), Puerto Morazan, Nicaragua (1989), Beira, Mozambique (1990) and Guangzhou, China (2001).

The story behind the first of these official partnerships, that of Bristol and Hannover, is an extraordinary tale of reconciliation, forgiveness and a friendship which has lasted for over seventy years.

125

In 1947 Bristol was in ruins. Six major Luftwaffe raids on the city had dropped a bombardment of almost 1,000 tons of high explosives and hundreds of incendiary bombs. 1,299 people were killed, over 80,000 houses were destroyed, and vast swathes of the city were little more than ash and rubble.

January of that year spread an unusually bitter winter across most of western Europe and few places were hit as ferociously as Germany. It was about this time that word reached the people of Bristol that many children in the city of Hannover could not attend school as their families were too poor to afford shoes. Soon afterwards, a handful of Bristolians began collecting donated shoes to be sent overseas.

Unsurprisingly, there was a degree of resentment among the population of the city. Bristol - and Britain at large - was experiencing an unprecedented period of austerity. Among the people of Bristol there was a general sentiment that the aggressors should be forced to fund the rebuilding of all cities that had been destroyed by German blitzes.

However, even those hardened against a nation that had been the sworn enemy of Britain only two years previously found some sympathy for the children of Hannover and within a month, thousands of pairs of shoes had been donated.

A party of four representatives from Bristol City Council were sent to Hannover to present the shoes to their counterparts in the city. While there, they were shown the extent of damage the Allied forces had inflicted on Hannover.

90% of Hannover's central district had been destroyed and attacks on residential areas had killed over 6,000 people and those who had survived were now struggling to live by slender means in the face of one of the harshest winters on record.

It was also noted that Bristol and Hannover were very similar in size and population and soon there was talk of the two cities being twinned. Later that year, dignitaries from Hannover arrived in Bristol and the two cities were officially united.

Bristol's act of charity towards Hannover is now seen as the very first post-war act of reconciliation to be organised by citizens themselves and it has led to a friendship that recently celebrated its 70th anniversary.

The two cities soon instigated a penpal programme where families in Bristol and Hannover would write to each other. The friendships forged through this letter exchange often lasted for decades, with second and even third generations of the families continuing the tradition.

Annually the cities arrange school exchanges, stage cultural events for representatives and exchange gifts at Christmas. Although Bristol is twinned with seven towns and cities across the globe (Hannover is also twinned with seven, including Hiroshima, Japan), it is said that none have been as important or long-lasting as that with Hannover - and it all began with a simple act of charity.

Looking out across Park Street you will notice a narrow church squeezed in along a row of shops. We are heading there next.

5. The Civic Peculiar

The small church opposite Bristol Cathedral is officially named St Mark's Church but is referred to by almost everybody as the Lord Mayor's Chapel.

It might not look like much from the outside, especially when contrasted with the sheer scale of the cathedral, but St Mark's Church has a surprisingly roomy and deep interior, despite being boxed in by buildings on three sides.

The church was built in 1230 when it was known as Gaunt's Chapel and was part of the Hospital of St Mark, which had opened in 1220. The hospital ran on charitable donations and offered free healthcare to those in desperate need. Being the 13th century, it's unlikely that any of these remedies helped in any way whatsoever, so the church often allowed patients the final solace of prayer before the inevitable happened.

In 1722, the highly unusual decision was taken by Bristol City Council (then known as the Bristol City Corporation) to buy the church so that it could serve as the primary place of worship for members of the city's administrative team. It was at this point that St Mark's became informally known as the Lord Mayor's Chapel.

When the church was bought by the city it was decreed that it would cease to align with any Christian denomination and over the years it has hosted congregations and services for Catholics, Anglicans, Quakers and others. It was the first religious building in Bristol to permit John Wesley to preach his newly established Methodist beliefs before he founded the New Room in 1739.

The unusual circumstances of the building's ownership means that it has been designated the title of "Civic

Peculiar", meaning that it belongs to neither a parish nor a denomination and instead is the property of the city's council itself. It is the only religious building in England to have such a title.

That concludes this brief walk around College Green. If you'd like to keep on exploring, head up Park Street until you come to a small set of steps on the right which lead to Frogmore Lane. The walk begins on page 169.

If you started this walk from the first half of the harbour tour, that walk resumes on page 43.

Walk Six
Picton Street

Picton Street

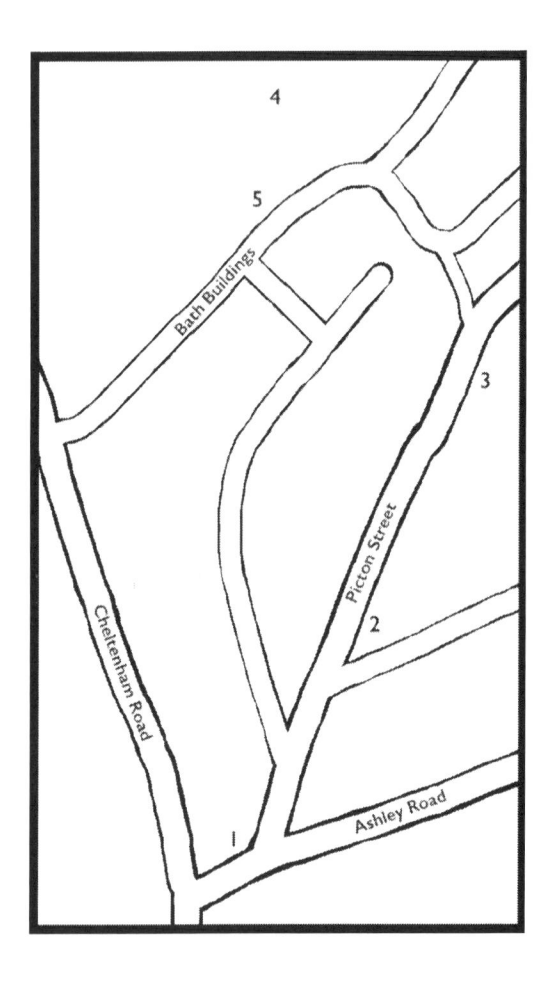

Picton Street has been described by the press as both "the hippest address in Britain" and "Bristol's most fascinating street". This simple, mostly downhill walk aims to show you why.

Over the course of a picturesque stroll through one of our city's true gems, I shall regale you with odd tales from the street's intriguing history, including debauched parties at a scandalous health resort, a lockup for the areas delinquents and even the home of Dracula himself…

This walk begins at the intersection of Cheltenham Road and Ashley Road.

1. The Stokes Croft and St Pauls Riots

Above a shop opposite the entry to Ashley Road there is an arresting piece of street art declaring "THINK LOCAL BOYCOTT TESCO" with an additional claim that "93% of local people say no to Tesco!" The origins of this graffiti lie in 2011 and the notorious Stokes Croft Riot.

Nowadays, many people assume that the confrontation was solely due to the opening of a branch of Tesco in the Stokes Croft area, which had been famed for its abundance of independent shops, but the actual spark began with the raiding of a squat.

Known as Telepathic Heights, the empty house near Picton Street had been home to a handful of squatters for over a year but a raid on the 21st of April 2011 led to its inhabitants being evicted in a manner which was described by some as "heavy-handed".

The police claimed that the reason for the raid was due to speculation that the squatters had been building petrol bombs to attack a branch of Tesco Express which had opened a few weeks previously.

Tensions in the area had been mounting, with many locals regarding the new store as another example of the counterculture and proudly independent personality of the area being taken over by bland corporations who were only interested in making money.

There was a fear that the commercial juggernaut would force independent traders to close throughout Stokes Croft and that the area would soon have all trace of its offbeat quirkiness ironed out. Although Tesco was not the only national brand to target the area, the Tesco Express on Cheltenham Road became an emblem of the turning tide towards corporate greed.

Word of the eviction of Telepathic Heights spread fast, with social media playing a large role in quickly organising a protest, and by 1.00am a standoff between the police and about 300 protestors had begun at the intersection between Ashley Road and Stokes Croft.

Bottles were thrown, riot shields were ripped out of officers hands, vehicles were overturned and fires were lit in wheelie bins along the street.

By about 3.00am most of the police left the scene, surmising that their presence was only inflaming the tensions. The rioters began to dissipate and by sunrise, Stokes Croft awoke to a scene of devastation.

The streets were littered with upturned cars, broken glass and smouldering embers. Opinions in the area were sharply divided between those who saw the riots as an outrage and those who saw them as a necessary act of civil disobedience.

The following weekend the riots resumed, but this time the participants targeted their ire more specifically towards the Tesco Express, which was completely vandalised.

The branch reopened a month later and though there were a few protests, the store has remained open ever since.

Of course, these were not the first riots the area had ever seen. On the night of the 2nd of April, 1980, police raided the notorious Black and White Cafe in St Pauls.

The premise had been described by the Guardian as "Britain's most dangerous hard drug den" and had been subjected to multiple raids before the night of what would come to be called "the St Paul's Riots".

The flashpoint for the raid becoming a riot is still debated but it may have been as simple as a police officer accidentally ripping a patron of the cafe's trousers and refusing to give him money to replace them.

This may seem like a trivial catalyst for a riot but tensions between police officers and the largely black residents of St Pauls had been simmering for years and the raid on the Black and White Cafe was enough for them to reach boiling point.

Over several hours the streets of St Paul's became the scene of a battle between rioters and police. Damage was caused to businesses around the area and emergency vehicles were vandalised.

The riot resulted in 25 people needing hospital treatment, 19 of whom were police officers, and the arrest of 130 people.

The Black and White Cafe went on to become the most raided premises in the country and it took an intervention by Parliament to force the Bristol police to scale back their targeting of the venue.

In 2003 Bristol City Council used a compulsory purchase order to forcibly buy the cafe from its owners and in 2005 the building was demolished and replaced by homes.

Looking down the hill to the bottom of Picton Street, there is a tall building on the right and opposite the Bristolian cafe. A plaque on the building proclaims that the actor Henry Irving once lived there. He will be the subject of our next stop.

2. Henry Irving

A plaque outside a grand looking building on Picton Street proudly boasts of its former resident, Henry Irving, and though his stay in Bristol was only brief, he would go on to become one of the most celebrated actors in British history.

Irving was born in 1838 into a working class family in the Somerset village of Keinton Mandeville. As a small child (and then known as John Henry Brodribb,) his family moved to Bristol so that his father, a salesman, could find work.

In 1842 the family settled in a house on Picton Street but the young boy did not take well to city life. At this time Bristol was dense with factories and lime kilns which darkened the sky and left a thin layer of soot over the streets and houses. Irving suffered greatly from breathing problems and after a few years, was sent to live with his aunt in the village of Halsetown in Cornwall.

Aged 13 he was sent to London to work for a law firm and began visiting theatres around the city. A performance of Hamlet with Samuel Phelps in the lead role sparked the boy's passion for performance and over the course of several years he wrote letters to actors and theatres across the country asking for work.

In 1856 he was given a position in a Sunderland theatre where he worked for many years before returning to London, now with a host of acting credits to his name. It was an 1871 performance of *The Bells* which launched him onto the West End scene but it was also the downfall of his personal life.

Following an argument with his wife of two years (who was pregnant with their second child) over his chosen profession, Irving leapt from the carriage they were being driven in and never saw his spouse again.

Eventually Irving would take control of the Lyceum Theatre, overseeing almost every aspect of its operation (and always casting himself as the lead). It was there that he became a close friend of the author Bram Stoker, who was a co-owner of the theatre. Irving's suave charm and charisma is said to have been a direct influence on Stoker in his creation of Count Dracula.

Rumoured to be a personal favourite of Queen Victoria, in 1895 Henry Irving became the first actor to be knighted. He retired soon afterwards and died in 1905.

Irving is only known to have visited Bristol a handful of times after becoming an actor, but that hasn't stopped rumours of his ghost haunting both the Bristol Old Vic and the Llandoger Trow. Although his time in the city was brief, it is a welcome connection to a legendary figure of the theatre world.

Henry Irving is not the only iconic actor associated with Picton Street. A young Archibald Leach briefly lived in a house further down the hill with his grandparents. His mother had been institutionalised at Glenside Mental Hospital and his father was an alcoholic, struggling to look after his son.

It was while living on Picton Street that Leach began working at Colston Hall's box office and got his first taste of the actor's life. Just a few years later he moved to America and changed his name to Cary Grant!

At the bottom of the hill there is a small, squat sandstone building with a letterbox built into one of its walls. This is where we're heading next.

3. The Charley Box

The Charley Box on Picton Street is one of the last to be found in Bristol, but at one time, they were dotted all about the city.

The cube-shaped building by the bottom of the hill was built in 1830 and served as a kind of lockup for the area's miscreants. The streets of Montpelier were dense with pubs and were often unruly at night. Bristol would not introduce an official police force until 1836 so areas of the city would attempt to keep their streets safe by funding private firms (sometimes even vigilante groups) to watch over the district.

In Montpelier this came in the form of a nightwatchman who would roam the streets at night. He was given the authority to apprehend wrongdoers, the majority of whom were drunk, and the intoxicated individual would be forced into the Charley Box overnight to sober up.

The following morning, he or she would be taken to a local magistrate whereupon the no doubt hungover Bristolian would have to plead for leniency.

The Charley Box consisted of two cells, one of which had manacles on the wall for particularly violent offenders who needed to be held in chains. The manacles can still be found inside the building.

There were once dozens of similar lockups all over the city but the one on Picton Street is the only one to remain in central Bristol. On Westbury Hill in the suburb of Westbury-on-Trym there is a similar cell, built into a wall, which served the same purpose.

The introduction of the police force led to a decline in the Charley Boxes' usage as the police had greater authority and were better funded than the nightwatchmen. The building is now privately owned and occasionally serves as an AirBnB residence for those brave enough to spend the night in a former cell.

Our next stop is the Old England pub. At the bottom of Picton Street, take a left onto Bath Buildings and follow it to the bend in the road where the pub's car park can be found.

4. W. G. Grace

The Old England pub has been part of Montpelier life since it was built in the latter half of the 18th century. Much like the ship of Theseus, Trigger's broom or the lineup of the Sugababes, the building has been expanded and rebuilt so many times that's it's unclear if any of the original structure may be part of the current pub.

From the early 1860s the venue became a favourite of the legendary cricketer W. G. Grace, who used the park at the back of the pub to hone his skills, eventually becoming the sport's first true all-rounder - proficient in batting, bowling, fielding and wicket-keeping.

William Gilbert Grace was born in Downend, which at the time was a small village on the outskirts of Bristol. His father, Henry Grace was a GP and his grandfather on his mother's side was the Bristol inventor George Pocock, famed for having created the Charvolent - a kind of kite driven carriage that was briefly popular in the 1820s (as well as a steam powered "spanking machine" capable of disciplining several unruly children at the same time).

Although Grace showed a proficiency for cricket from a young age (as did two of his brothers, E. M. And Fred Grace, who also went on to become semi-professional cricketers) he believed that truly exceptional sportsmen were not born but "made by coaching and practice".

Grace enrolled at Bristol Medical College aged 20 but it would take him 11 years to finally qualify, due to various cricketing diversions.

W. G. Grace's other great passion in life was drinking and he was notorious for the copious amount of beer he could consume with seemingly no effect on his ability to play cricket. It is said that the Old England pub was as much a draw for its ale as it was for its pub garden, where Grace would attract huge crowds to watch him play on summer evenings.

Although he technically remained an amateur cricketer, due to his medical practice, it was said that he earned far more from his sporting commitments than he ever did as a physician.

His achievements in the sport are almost unrivalled, with 44 seasons to his name and countless records. It has been said that Grace was not just the first true cricketing icon, but the world's first celebrity sportsperson. Appearances by Grace were guaranteed to draw a crowd - the 6' 2" giant of a man with a fiercely competitive temper made for quite a spectacle.

Grace retired from cricket in 1908, aged 60, and died of a heart attack seven years later. He has been memorialised at cricketing venues across the country and the Old England proudly continues its connection to the great sportsman with the mural of a cricketer on its frontage and also by being (probably) the only pub in England with full-sized cricket practice nets in its garden.

Turning around from the Old England you will see Montpelier Health Centre - the last stop on this walk.

5. The Rennison Baths

Throughout the Georgian era, the people of Britain turned health crazy. Whether it was crash dieting, exercises at dawn or a belief in the benefits of copious gin consumption, there was no wellbeing fad that could not find support in parts of society.

One of the most abiding of all of these was the belief in the health giving properties of bathing. Often it was believed that the waters themselves had some kind of medicinal qualities - a belief exploited by the city of Bath and its natural spring waters - but there was a general understanding that bathing was a path to better health.

Of course bathing and general cleanliness were a way of distinguishing the upper class of society from the lower orders. Bathing was time consuming and therefore impractical for workers with very little free time. As a result, the activity had a certain sophistication about it.

Unsurprisingly, there were plenty of entrepreneurs hoping to lure the wealthy elite with privately owned bathing pools and one such person was Thomas Rennison who, in 1764, bought a large mill pool which once stood where Montpelier Health Centre can now be found.

The pool was enclosed away from prying eyes behind a wall and an entry fee was charged by Rennison. It was immediately successful. So much so that the businessman set about landscaping the grounds around the pool into pleasure gardens, including a bowling green and a coffee house. The Old England pub was also built to be part of this complex.

Being situated just outside of what was then the city boundary, it was not subject to the same laws as Bristol and as such, there was an air of scandal about the place, with both men and women sharing the pool - and men occasionally bathing naked. Later on, a purpose built pool for the use of women only was provided.

Whether anything truly scandalous went on at the Rennison Baths will probably never be known but every year a somewhat debauched party was held at the site. Known as the "Bean Feast", it was a celebration of excess with drunken revelries going on well into the night.

It was also something of a parody of civic formalities associated with Bristol, with each feast culminating in the election of a mayor and a sheriff of the party, who were sworn in with ludicrous ceremony to much hilarity.

With time (and the invention of home plumbing) the fashion for communal bathing faded away, as did the visitors to the Rennison Baths, but the pools continued to be privately owned and used until 1916 when the land was sold to Colston Girls' School. The pool was covered over but part of the gardens remained until 1978 when the last piece of available land was sold to Montpelier Health Centre, which still stands to this day.

That is the last stop on this walk. If you joined this tour as an alternative route on the Central Bristol walk, head towards Broadmead and John Wesley's New Room and then turn to page 105.

Walk Seven
St Michael's Hill

St Michael's Hill

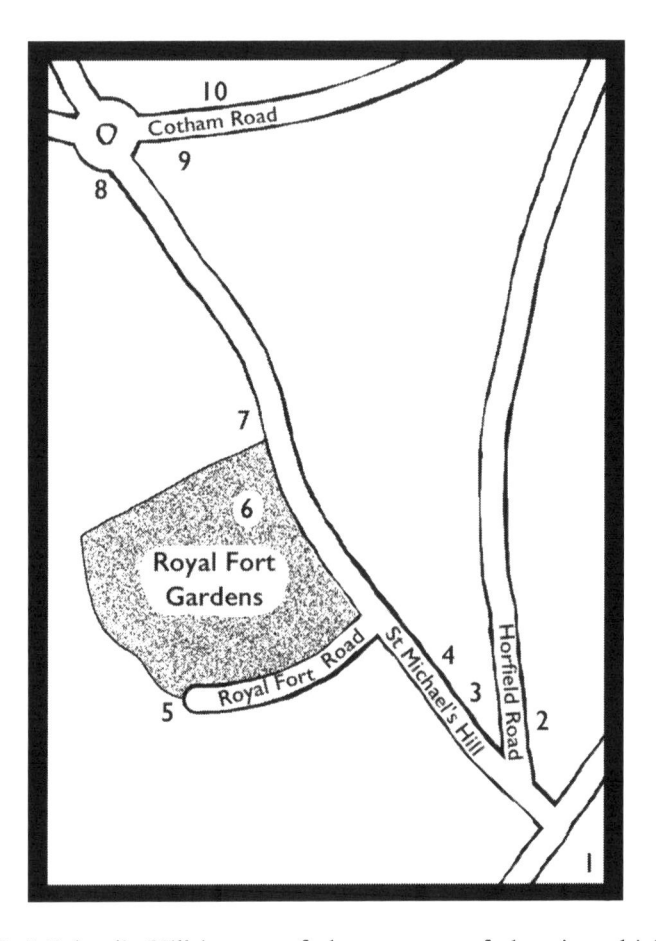

St Michael's Hill is one of those areas of the city which is *dense* with history, yet its importance to the city has often been overlooked in modern times - that is something I hope to rectify somewhat with this walk.

This is easily one of the most challenging walks in this book. The hill is very steep and goes on for quite some time, but there are plenty of stops along the way.

On St Michael's Hill we'll encounter one of the most divisive figures in Bristol history, the birthplace of an acting dynasty and the site of a battle which turned the fates of a war around…

This walk begins at the Foster's Almshouses, which is the pretty set of buildings beside a church at the top of Christmas Steps.

1. Foster's Almshouses

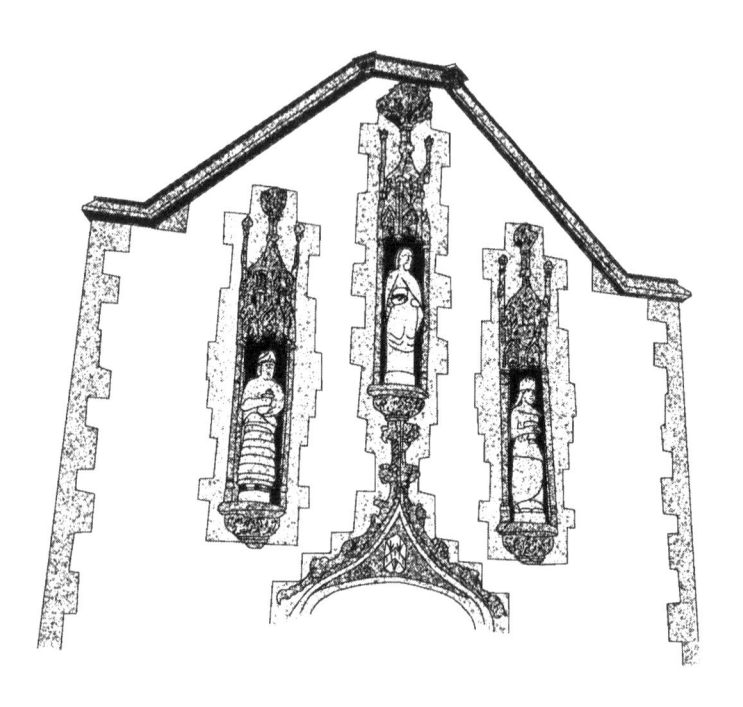

The charming collection of small houses around a courtyard garden at the top of Christmas Steps is actually the third set of almshouses to stand on the site.

The original was built following the death of the Bristol merchant John Foster, who bequeathed a good deal of money in his will so that a series of buildings could be built to house the destitute and infirm. Foster had made his fortune trading salt around Iceland.

His almshouses were similar in design to what can be found today, including a small chapel for use of the residents which backs onto Christmas Steps. His original design featured representations of the three "wise men" of the Nativity story, leading some to speculate that the original chapel may have given the steps their name (although a more commonly believed reason is that it is a corruption of the word "Knifesmiths" meaning knife maker - a common occupation in the area.)

Almshouses have played an important role in the history of the city and provided free or inexpensive housing for the underprivileged, or in some cases, retired workers who had been employed by wealthy merchants. The houses were seen as an act of charity which also had the benefit of ensuring that the financier would earn some extra kudos on arrival at the gates of Heaven.

The almshouses were rebuilt again in 1708 and once more between 1861 and 1883 - these are the buildings which remain to this day. The architects were the well-known duo of Foster and Wood and the final stage of their construction was an approximation of the original chapel.

Their design had three niches that were intended to house depictions of the three wise men but for reasons which seem to have been lost to time, the statues were not added until 1962 when the buildings underwent a restoration process.

The sculptors were Ernest Pascoe and John Huggins who not only crafted the three figures (each bears a gift for the newborn Christ child) but added a single star over them to represent the one the wise men were "following yonder", according to the New Testament story.

The collection of buildings ceased to operate as almshouses in 2007 when it was decided that the mostly elderly and infirm residents were struggling with the crooked staircases and narrow corridors so the buildings were sold as private homes.

In 2009, the residents were moved into a new, purpose built block of almshouses in Henbury which is run by Bristol Charities, an organisation established to help the poor and vulnerable which was established in 1833 but has its roots in the 14th century and has helped countless Bristolians in search of healthcare, food and shelter.

Head up the stone steps towards Perry Road. Turn right and follow the road up to the foot of St Michael's Hill on the left. Head upwards until you reach Horfield Road where you will find a sporting goods shop called Easy Runner.

2. The Redgrave Dynasty

On the 22nd of March, 1908 a boy was born in a house on an ordinary Bristol Street. The house is now Easy Runner on Horfield Road and the boy was Michael Redgrave - who would go on to be the patriarch of one of the most prominent acting families in the world.

Michael was not the first of his family to become an actor. His mother, Mary Scudamore, appeared both on the stage and screen and his father, Roy Redgrave, was a silent movie actor.

Roy abandoned his wife when she was pregnant with Michael to look for acting work in Australia. Michael was raised by his mother and never met his father - the family did not even know that he had died in 1922 until many years later.

He began pursuing an acting career at Clifton College and after a brief stint as a teacher, found work as part of a theatre ensemble in Liverpool. It was while working here that he met his wife, Rachel, a stage actor touring with the Royal Shakespeare Company. They married in 1935 and went on to have three children, Vanessa, Corin and Lynn - all three subsequently became actors.

Of the three siblings, Vanessa is the only one to have been awarded the "Triple Crown of Acting" - all three American acting awards - an Oscar, an Emmy and a Tony. She went on to have Natasha and Joely Richardson with her husband, the director Tony Richardson. Both of Vanessa's offspring would go on to have successful acting careers, although Natasha's would be cut tragically short following a fatal skiing accident in 2009.

Corin Redgrave forged a prestigious career for himself on the stage, playing a host of notable roles, but it was for his radical, far-left activism that he wished to be remembered. He helped co-found the UK Marxist Party with his sister Vanessa, which went on to become the short-lived Peace and Progress Party. His daughter, Jemma Redgrave, is an actor perhaps best known for a semi-recurring role in Doctor Who.

Corin died in 2010, aged 70.

Lynn Redgrave was a highly-regarded actor of stage and screen and though greatly respected in her profession is unique in being the only person in history to have been nominated for all categories of the EGOT (or "Big Four") American entertainment awards - Emmy, Grammy, Oscar and Tony - without winning a single category.

Lynn married the actor John Clark in 1967 and a tabloid sensation was caused in the year 2000 when Clark had an affair with Redgrave's personal assistant, which resulted in the birth of a child. The assistant would go on to marry one of Redgrave's children, causing further scandal. Lynn died in 2010.

The Redgrave acting dynasty may have had only a short-lived link to the city, but it was an important one. A blue plaque on the outside of Easy Runner is testament to our city's tie to this prestigious lineage. With Daisy Bevan, the daughter of Joely Richardson and Tim Bevan becoming the first of a fifth generation of the Redgrave family to pursue an acting career, it could be a legacy which goes on for years to come.

Return to St Michael's Hill and follow it upwards. On the right is the Colston Arms, which will be our next stop.

3. The Colston Arms

In recent years the legacy of Edward Colston, the Bristol merchant who made a huge amount of money through the slave trade, has been highly questioned. Along with this has come a great deal of pondering as to why so many schools, roads and venues have been named after him - and why they persist on operating under a name which is associated with slavery.

One such establishment is the Colston Arms on St Michael's Hill, which is why it may come as a surprise to hear that the pub was actually involved in one of the boldest acts of civil disobedience in support of racial integration Bristol has ever seen.

America joined the Second World War in 1942. There had been a general mood of resentment among the Allied forces that the nation should have intervened sooner but when troops began arriving across Britain, they were mostly welcomed and treated well.

Not that the resentments stopped entirely. The Americans wore sharp uniforms and had well-stocked rations and spoke with a glamorous accent most Bristolians had only ever heard at the cinema.

However, like they were while in America, the troops stationed in Bristol were kept segregated along racial lines. This meant that streets and venues were designated as white or "coloured" by US officials.

That Bristol fell in line with these rules is disappointing but the Americans represented such hope for the Allied forces that there was pressure to acquiesce to whatever demands they made while staying in Britain.

It's not known which establishment in Bristol was the first to break the colour bar, but the one most commonly named is the Colston Arms. If it was not the first it was certainly one of the very earliest - and it is possible that the pub simply refused to follow the rules on segregation to begin with and never turned anyone away on grounds of race.

Had it been a single establishment - or even just a handful of them that had defied this order - there would probably have been severe penalties, but within a matter of months, almost all pubs around central Bristol were openly defying the order and doing so in such numbers that the US officials were powerless to stop it.

It may seem like a small victory when faced with the extraordinary intolerance black and minority ethnic American soldiers would face in their own country, but it was a meaningful one. Bristol not only refused to segregate but stood up to authority in a manner which has defined our fiercely independent minded (and often rebellious) city throughout history.

Next door to the Colston Arms is another establishment bearing the merchant's name. The Colston Almshouses is a grand, U-shaped terrace of buildings and is the next stop on this walk.

4. The Colston Almshouses

The pleasant, uniform and almost entirely symmetrical complex of homes called the Colston Almshouses was completed in 1691. It was built as a permanent residence for 12 men - all retired seamen who had worked for the Bristol born merchant and slave trader Edward Colston - and 16 women, mostly widows who might otherwise have been destitute and living on the streets.

The buildings were restored in 1861 and 1988 but unlike the Fosters Almshouses, most of the original design remains intact.

When the houses were first built, a private chapel was placed in the centre of the design and it was a condition of all residents' stay that they must attend at least twice a day, with a bell sounding atop the chapel when the mandatory services began. In the following years these rules were relaxed somewhat, first to three services a week and later only on Sundays.

The walls of the chapel are lined with wood which was salvaged from ships that were due to be dismantled, which has led to a long-standing rumour that some of these vessels belonged to Edward Colston and served as slave ships.

By 1691 Colston was 55, living in London, and the most senior executive in the Royal African Company which transferred goods from Bristol and London to west African ports in exchange for slaves who were then shipped to America (in squalid, often fatal conditions) where they were forced to work on plantations and the goods produced there brought back to England.

It made Colston tremendously wealthy and with this money he established several schools, hospitals and almshouses in Bristol and London. When the almshouses on St Michael's Hill were built, the entire fleet of Colston's ships were in service across the Atlantic, so it's unlikely that any of the timber lining the chapel's walls came from vessels involved in the slave trade.

Edward Colston's legacy is one Bristolians have struggled to reckon with over the years. A man who was capable of both acts of charity and barbaric greed, he will likely remain the most controversial figure our city has ever had.

Continue up the hill until you reach the turning onto Royal Fort Road. Follow
the wall on your right as it runs parallel to the road until you reach a gatehouse named Prince Rupert's gate.

5. Bristol and the Civil War

During the English Civil War (1642-1651) Bristol was of immense strategic importance. Second only to London in wealth, it was also perfectly situated for international trade. There was a general belief among both the Royalists and the Parliamentarians that whoever managed to secure Bristol would secure victory.

There is no doubt that Bristol was fully aware of its own significance and as such played a rather calculated game. The city hosted dignitaries from both sides of the conflict in an attempt to appear superficially neutral but also to curry favour with whichever side appeared to be winning at the time.

Although usually referred to simply as the English Civil War, the conflict actually came in three waves, with brief periods of peace in-between. The Royalists, or Cavaliers, fought on behalf of Charles I and the absolute authority of the monarchy, while the Parliamentarians, or Roundheads, wanted power to rest in the hands of elected representatives.

Less than a year into the war, Bristol witnessed its first major battle. On the morning of the 26th of July a Royalist battalion laid siege to a garrison near to where Bristol Museum is now, and in doing so, claimed the city for Charles I and those loyal to the monarchy.

The Royalists set about building a huge, pentagonal fort overlooking the city as well as barracks for the substantial army they had stationed there. Their control of the city was short-lived however, as on the 11th of September 1645 an assault on the fort led by the Parliamentarians not only led to a great deal of bloodshed on both sides, but the Royalists surrendering and essentially handing control of Bristol to the Roundheads.

The taking of Bristol is seen as one of the major turning points in the English Civil War and though the conflict would go on for some considerable time longer, by the following year Charles I was practically powerless and on the run.

Prince Rupert's Gate which stands high and proud over Royal Fort Road is named after Prince Rupert of the Rhine who led the Cavalier charge into Bristol in 1643 and this gatehouse is the only substantial portion of the fort the Royalists built in the city.

Excavations in 2001 and 2009 around the gatehouse found underground chambers, probably used for gunpowder storage, and evidence of settlements which could have housed hundreds of soldiers as well as cannonballs from the Civil War.

The tranquil green space of Royal Fort Gardens is now a lush and beautiful city park, so much so that it's almost impossible to imagine that it was not just the scene of incredible violence, but also played a vital role in the shaping of British history.

Go through the gate into Royal Fort Gardens. There will be a set of steps on your right and at the top you should be able to see a section of freestanding wall in the middle of an open square.

6. The Ivy Gate

Standing as something of curiosity in the middle of a campus piazza, the Ivy Gate is a red brick section of wall with a metal gate built into it. Seemingly nonsensical at first, this wall was once the opening to lavish gardens.

Thomas Tyndall was a Bristol banker who had profited greatly by investing in the slave trade. In 1753 he bought a plot of land where this walled gate - known as the Ivy Gate - now stands. Over the following 14 years he would buy up surrounding fields to create one of the largest personal estates in the city at the time.

The land also featured the Civil War era fortification that had been built by the Cavaliers but taken by the Roundheads in 1646. A hundred years on from the war, the structure had not stood the test of time and was looking rather tumbledown and weathered. Tyndall had the building demolished and a grand house built in its place.

He named the house Fort Royal in honour of the fortification and the building still exists - now Royal Fort - and is used as the University of Bristol Faculty of Science offices.

The Ivy Gate was built in 1758 and led into an ornate, walled garden where it is believed there was at least two glasshouses (an excavation in 2009 revealed that a further two glass houses were built nearby, as well as an underground icehouse.)

In 1799, Thomas Tyndall, son of the previous owner of the estate, funded extensive landscaping by the renowned gardener Humphry Repton, and many of the trees around the park are believed to have been part of his original design.

On the outside wall of one of the faculty buildings there is proof of how this tradition of grandiose gardening has continued to this day, in the form of a vertical garden, consisting of 11 different varieties of plants. It's a stunning use of space and really worth looking out for.

With your back to Royal Fort House, continue past the Ivy Gate and head down some steps which lead onto St. Michael's Hill. Take a left and just after you have passed a zebra crossing, you should be able to see a peculiar structure built into the pavement that looks something like a tiny lighthouse or a very skinny Dalek.

7. The Street Vents

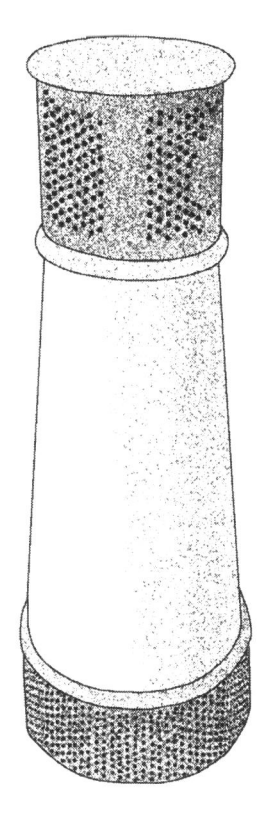

When I started @WeirdBristol Twitter feed back in 2017, I had no idea of two things - firstly, that there were so many people interested in the lesser-known history of the city as I was, and secondly, that it would have such a profound effect on my understanding of Bristol.

Suddenly I was walking the streets with a keen eye for anything unusual or out of place, spotting peculiarities in familiar places and I realised I'd been walking past a feature of our city countless times over the years without ever once questioning or even noticing them.

The curious little structures which can be found in dozens of locations throughout Bristol look like little lighthouses, but stand unassumingly on pavements from Bedminster to Redland. While they might at first seem a mystery, the clue to their purpose can be found nearby - a metal, double-doored opening built into the street which will always be just a few feet away.

Although it's often assumed that they're traffic bollards (or, according to one online discussion board, ashtrays), they're actually vents for underground power substations.

Beneath Bristol there is not just a vast network of caves, waterways and man-made mines but also a web of electric and gas supply lines, each requiring substations to serve as junction points to reroute power to different parts of the city.

The doors in the pavement serve as entryways to these substations and the strange structures above ground help vent heat to prevent them from becoming too hot to operate - which is why they can feel noticeably warm on winter days.

It may not be the most revolutionary or important feature of the streets of Bristol, but I guarantee that once you've seen one, you'll start spotting them everywhere!

We're continuing uphill. Follow the St Michael's Hill past Highbury Vaults, which will be on your right, and towards the roundabout where the road meets Cotham Hill, Cotham Road and Hampton Road.

8. The St Michael's Hill Gallows

The seemingly ordinary roundabout at the top of St Michael's Hill seems like an unlikely place to be the scene of countless gruesome deaths, but from the early 1700s, this spot was the location of the city's gallows.

Just outside of the boundary of Bristol, the gallows were kept up all year round as a permanent reminder to those coming into the city of what would happen to them if they broke the law.

By the 18th century, hangings had become an enormous public spectacle, with often hundreds of people attending. So popular were these executions that the newspapers published times, dates and the names of those due to be hanged in full-paged articles, emphasising their terrible crimes and encouraging onlookers to attend as part of the civic duty of all law-abiding people.

Executions were usually carried out in batches, with several criminals meeting the noose on the same day. The most notorious hanging in Bristol's history happened on the 3rd of September, 1736.

Joshua Harding and John Vernon were both burglars and house breakers, and though unknown to one another in their criminal careers, were to be united forever in history due to the astonishing tale of their hangings.

They were both due to be hanged in the early afternoon and were brought from their cells in Newgate Prison (where the Galleries shopping centre can be found nowadays) a few hours before, so that they may make their peace with God and be served a final meal. Contrary to popular opinion, this did not happen at the Highbury Vaults, as that pub did not exist at the time.

As expected, a huge crowd had gathered to witness not just the executions of Harding and Vernon, but about half a dozen others.

All the executions were carried out as planned, including those of the two thieves, but after the bodies were cut down and placed into coffins on the back of a cart Vernon began to move and gasp for air. Vernon would die later that evening from his injuries but during his brief revival he was capable of speaking and shaking hands with acquaintances.

Astonishingly, on the same journey back from the gallows, Harding too began to show signs of life and later that day was claimed to be on his feet and walking again.

A hasty judgement from a magistrate was that Harding had received the punishment he had been sentenced to and that the law had been carried out to the letter. The magistrate did not go as far as granting the man his freedom however, and he was instead transported to a convict colony in either Australia or America.

Although it may seem a pleasant enough spot today, the roundabout atop St Michael's Hill is said to, on occasion, echo with the chilling screams of countless men and women being brought to the gallows centuries before.

The church beside the roundabout is Cotham Parish Church. On the north side of the building there is a memorial plaque dedicated to the five Bristol martyrs who were executed nearby.

9. The Bristol Martyrs

A plaque on an outside wall of Cotham Parish Church serves as a permanent memorial for the five men who were executed on St Michael's Hill during the reign of the queen who history would name "Bloody Mary".

Mary I came to power when her younger brother, Edward VI died - aged only 15. Edward had attempted to prevent either of his sisters becoming the monarch following his death, fearing that either Mary or Elizabeth would fracture the country, and instead requested that his successor would be his cousin, Lady Jane Grey.

Following his death, there was a period of turmoil while it was decided who should wear the crown and, after the beheading of Lady Jane Grey, it was determined that Mary was the rightful heir.

As was expected (and feared by Edward VI) the staunchly Catholic Mary decreed that the entire nation should fall in line with her religious beliefs and that the Church of England, which her father had established, would cease to exist in her realm.

The Bristol Martyrs were five Protestant men living in the city who were all executed for refusing to deny their beliefs. Between October of 1555 and August 1557 they were killed in the most terrifying and gruesome manner imaginable - being burned to death.

The five men were Thomas Banion, Thomas Hale, William Shapton, Richard Sharp and Edward Sharpe, and the crime for which they were executed was blasphemy, in this case refusing to declare that the Sacrament - a consecrated piece of bread or cracker - was the actual physical flesh of Christ.

The executions were carried out on the spot where the roundabout now stands. In 1556, Richard Sharp was intended to be executed on the same afternoon as Edward Sharpe, but upon being brought to pyre, broke down in tears and denounced his Protestant faith. He was allowed to go free but was executed the following year after once again refusing to acknowledge the Sacrament.

The Bristol Martyrs were not alone in dying for their beliefs. During Mary's five year reign it's believed that as many as 300 Protestants were burned to death. Among them were women and children. The plaque on the wall of Cotham Parish Church serves as a reminder not just of the five men's devotion but of the ultimate and ghastly cost of religious intolerance of all kinds.

On the low wall surrounding Cotham Church (on the Cotham Road side) there is a small plaque marking the former location of Bewell's Cross. It is the next stop of this tour.

10. Bewell's Cross

Cotham Parish Church was completed in 1843 - making it a relative baby compared to Bristol's oldest churches and religious buildings, but a single stone in its surrounding wall is far older and a relic of the old city boundary.

On the Cotham Road side of the church wall there is a plaque informing passersby that the large stone beneath it was once part of Bewell's Cross.

Not a great deal is known about this cross, aside from that it was built in 1373 and once stood atop St Michael's Hill when the whole area was open meadowland. Its purpose was to mark the boundary of the city and the county of Gloucestershire beyond (a boundary which has subsequently moved greatly).

The importance of city boundaries may not seem all that relevant nowadays, but for centuries the residents of Bristol would have been subject to the specific laws and tolls of the city and visitors would be expected to abide by them. For the most part these would be the general laws of the country but specific details involving things such as market trading, public drinking and even animal care were unique to many towns and cities.

The name Bewell's Cross is a mysterious one and its origins are not clear. However, it has been suggested that it could be a corruption of the name *Beowulf* - an uncommon surname but one which was recorded in the area at the time.

The cross was removed sometime in the 19th century for reasons which have been lost to time but this single stone was repurposed to build the wall around Cotham Church, and though the original monument was probably destroyed, this little relic serves as an interesting memory of a Bristol long, long ago.

That concludes this walk up St Michael's Hill. This is one of the most challenging walks in the book so I think you've deserved a pint or a snack! I recommend the nearby Highbury Vaults, not just for its terrific menu but also for its lovely pub garden, which is, in my opinion, one of the finest and most unusual in Bristol!

Walk Eight
Bristol Miscellany

Bristol Miscellany

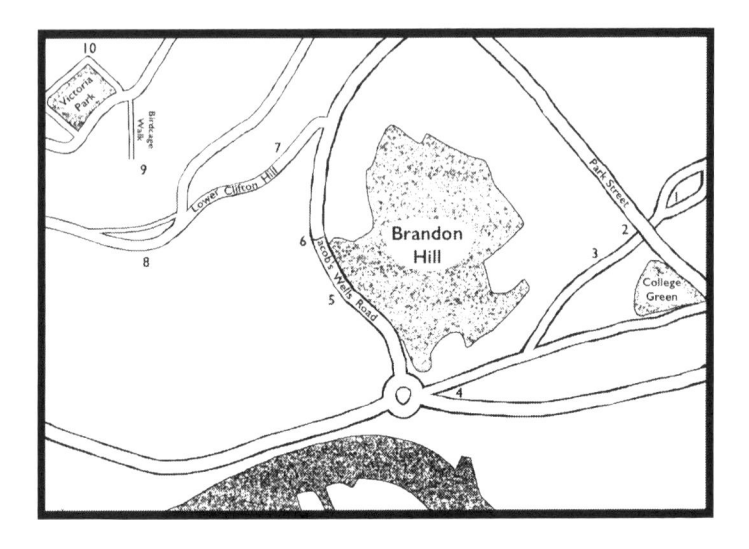

This chapter is a bit unusual as it's a walk which consists of all the bits and pieces that I couldn't get to fit into any of the other walks! As a result, it's a trivia trove of bits and pieces across the city.

This the longest and most challenging walk in the book, but don't let that put you off, as there are some fascinating stops along the way!

You will find a pioneering doctor who founded her own surgery, an ancient holy site which was almost lost forever and an incredible story of destruction and survival in a long-gone Clifton church…

This walk begins outside the Hatchet Inn, on the side of the pub which faces the Queenshilling.

1. Plant a Tree in '73

On a patch of ground beside the Hatchet Inn (on the side facing the Queenshilling) there is a large tree. It is a Norway Maple and though it may look like countless other trees that can be found throughout Bristol, the story of how it came to be here is a rather interesting one.

The tree was planted in 1973 as part of a government backed initiative called "Plant a Tree in '73" Britain's elm tree population had been devastated by the spread of Dutch elm disease and by the early '70s there were concerns that the species could be completely wiped out.

The disease was first identified in 1910 in the Netherlands but is believed to have originated in Asia, where the trees had evolved to be more resistant to it. Until the 1940s the disease - which is caused by a toxic form of fungi carried by beetles, had travelled only slowly across Europe and North America - and most trees were able to recover - but a new, far more virulent strain which emerged in the late 1960s arrived in the UK soon afterwards and began devastating the nation's elm tree population.

This new strain had an almost 100% fatality rate and within just a few years, most of Britain's elm trees were either dead or dying.

Plant a Tree in '73 began as an effort by conservationists to replace the trees with species that were resistant to the disease and soon had the support of the government and local councils. A majority of the tree planting was carried out by schools or volunteers.

The tree beside the Hatchet was the first in Bristol to be planted as part of the initiative and over the course of the year (and the year after, as part of a campaign called "Plant Some More in '74") thousands of new trees were established across the city.

The nationwide campaign was enormously successful and led to an estimated 160,000 trees being planted throughout the UK. Britain may have lost the majority of its elm trees, but this effort ensured that the country and its wildlife would not suffer this loss too greatly.

Heading past the Queenshilling, go under Park Street via the bridge and take the stone steps on the left. About halfway up you should be looking at the Mauretania building on Park Street and its neon sign depicting a ship.

2. The Mauretania

Overlooking Frog Lane and Park Street, the Mauretania Public House has been a popular icon of the city for decades. The flashing neon sign depicting RMS Mauretania had been switched off for many years but in 2018 it was fully restored and can now be seen in operation every night.

The original building was constructed in 1870 but an expansion in 1938 more than doubled its size. It was also in 1938 that the neon sign was installed and became the first in Bristol to have a "moving" feature, where alternating lights create the illusion of movement.

The public house takes its name from the RMS Mauretania, the opulent ocean liner which was launched in 1906 and heralded a new standard for refinement and luxury in transatlantic crossings - and was the largest and fastest cruise liner of her age.

She was the sister ship to RMS Lusitania, the ill-fated vessel which was torpedoed in 1915 by a German U-boat, drawing America into WWI. Mauretania herself was repurposed during the war, operating as an armed cruiser and later a hospital ship. She was repainted grey to make her less conspicuous on the open sea but her sheer size made her unsuitable for military campaigns and she spent most of WWI in a dry dock.

RMS Mauretania returned to service as a cruise liner after the war and remained in operation until 1935. Over her career she was surpassed in both size and speed but few ships could claim to be as luxurious, which is why following the scrapping, many of her original fixtures were brought to Bristol and became part of the Mauretania Public House interior.

A large section of the ship's first class lounge now serves as the building's bar, with original mahogany panelling from her library lining the walls.

When the neon sign was switched on again in 2018 there was a great deal of celebration from Bristolians, who had fondly remembered the lighting feature. The sign now serves as a cheerful remnant of 1930s Bristol and also a reminder of the building's unusual ties to one of the greatest and most famous ships in history.

Continue along Frog Lane and head right at the junction. There is a large building here facing the car park. Known as Brunel House, this building is the next stop on this tour.

3. Brunel House

The area surrounding Brunel House on St George's Road may not be the most picturesque corner of Bristol, with a car park occupying most of the space and the rather unattractive rear facade of City Hall looming over it, but the building itself is a rather special curio and was once part of an audacious scheme that would permit travel to America in a way that had never been seen before.

The building was opened as the Great Western Steamship Hotel in 1839 and although most of the design is attributed to Richard Shackleton Pope (whose distinct style can be found across Bristol, including the Freemasons' Hall and the Arnolfini) the two protruding archways on the front of the building were based on sketches by Isambard Kingdom Brunel.

The hotel itself was the idea of Brunel and was an important step in his plan for a fully-integrated system of travel between London and New York.

Trains would begin at London's Paddington station and would bring travellers to Bristol Temple Meads via the Great Western Railway. Brunel would have designed every major step of this journey to this point.

From Temple Meads, people would be brought to The Great Western Steamship Hotel by horse and cart and the following morning they would begin their voyage to New York aboard what was then Brunel's greatest achievement - the SS Great Western.

This seamless form of travel even had stables for horses overnight so that they could take passengers and their luggage directly to the steamship. If you peer through the arch on the right side you can make out a large open space in a courtyard with towering walls on three sides that served as a kind of "horse hotel" within the structure itself. It was known as the horse bazaar, and to mark its unusual history, a statue of a man and a horse can just about be seen through the arch.

Brunel's plan for integrated travel was successful for a few years but the SS Great Western was put out of service in 1846. By this time the SS Great Britain had proven to be a much more reliable means of crossing the Atlantic but her journey to New York departed from Liverpool. Soon the Great Western Steamship Hotel was operating as any other hotel in the city and was later bought as administrative offices for the council.

It now serves as rather swanky student accommodation but the grounds are opened on certain days and I highly recommend having a look around, as the gardens have been landscaped in such a way as t0 be a haven for urban wildlife, including bee-friendly planting and numerous bird boxes.

Continue along St George's Road. Once you come to the top of a small hill, turn right and follow the road until you reach a roundabout at the bottom of Jacob's Wells Road. At the intersection between St George's Road and Anchor road, there is a red, triangular building, on it there is a plaque which states it is the "Read Dispensary." This is our next stop.

4. Eliza Walker Dunbar

The red, wedge shaped building at the foot of Jacob's Wells Road was designed in 1905 and opened in 1906 to serve as the second home of the revolutionary Read Dispensary - a medical facility specifically for women where they could have a consultation with, and receive treatments from, a female doctor.

The dispensary was the mastermind of Dr Eliza Walker Dunbar, one of the first women in British history to qualify as a doctor.

Born Eliza Louisa Walker in Hyderabad, India in 1845, her father worked as a doctor for the Bombay Military Department. As she grew up she began to express an interest in medicine but found that no medical schools would take her application to study there seriously.

She instead paid for private tuition and later travelled to Switzerland to complete her education and in doing so became one of the "Zurich Seven" - seven women who graduated from the University of Zurich with a medical degree at the same time. Walker did so in 1872 with a special distinction.

She returned to England and applied for work at several institutions and was eventually accepted at the Bristol Royal Hospital for Sick Children in 1873. Her presence led to the seven male doctors who were employed there all walking out - leaving Walker as the sole practitioner of the hospital for five days until she, with no other option, resigned from the post.

Now going by the name of Dr Eliza Walker Dunbar she opened a private facility in Clifton, known as the Read Dispensary for Women and Children, and by 1877 there were five other female doctors working alongside her.

By 1904 the Read Dispensary had almost 2,500 registered patients and the hall where the facility had originally been set up was being threatened with demolition for road expansion, so a plot of land was bought on St George's Road for a replacement to be built.

The building itself was designed by the Bristol-based architect Percival Hartland Thomas in the architectural style known as Domestic Revival. This style was popular in the 19th and 20th centuries and was a revival of the ornate and welcoming homes associated with the reign of Queen Anne.

The Read Dispensary was funded by charitable donations from across the city (and country) and provided a vital service for women and children, many of whom were from underprivileged backgrounds. Elizabeth Walker Dunbar continued working at and funding the practice until her death in 1925 at the age of 80. The building now stands as a testament to her bravery and tenacity.

We're heading up the hill. At about the halfway between the roundabout at the bottom and the turning onto Constitution Hill, there is a large block of flats called Brandon House. On the front of the building, towards the lower side of the hill, there is a blue plaque marking the former site of Jacob's Well Theatre.

5. Jacob's Well Theatre

Throughout Bristol's long history its boundaries have altered greatly. Swelling outwards, not just as its population has risen, but as it has demanded better quality housing. In doing so, the city stretched to encompass surrounding towns and villages, most of which still bear the names of when they were independent settlements, like Clifton and Bedminster.

During the 18th century the city hadn't quite encompassed the area of Hotwells and it sat just outside of the city boundary. For this reason, it was chosen as the home of one of the earliest theatres in the area.

Theatre had, for a long time, been associated with crass, unruly and often drunken behaviour. It was one of the few places where the upper and lower classes would go for entertainment alongside one another and as such, had an air of scandal about it among the social elite.

Moreover, female performers had only been permitted onto the stage since the Restoration period and there was a suspicion that any woman who could feign intimacy or romance on stage was likely also a sex worker - a not entirely ungrounded assumption as most actors were severely underpaid and often had to find other means of getting by than their performance fees alone.

The theatre was located outside of the city border so that it could be beyond the jurisdiction of Bristol and therefore beyond the prying eyes of the puritanical city leaders.

It was never a fine theatre. It was small and gloomy and the stage was only a little larger than a standard dinner table. If an actor had to leave on one side of the stage and re-enter on another, they would have to run around the building to a door on the other side to do so.

Nevertheless, the theatre was popular and a sold out performance could earn its investors a great deal of money. It was not without its problems though, as rich people who were brought to the playhouse from Clifton and Queen Square had to pass through the mostly lawless streets of Hotwells and there were fears that in doing so they were vulnerable to muggers and thieves.

As a solution, the theatre hired link-boys, who would guide people home through the dark streets with a burning torch for the fee of one farthing.

Despite being surpassed in size and grandeur by the opening of the Theatre Royal (now the Bristol Old Vic) in 1766, the Jacob's Well Theatre continued in operation until 1799. Its final performance is believed to have been a pantomime.

Following its closure the building was likely abandoned and later demolished. Though it's not known precisely where the little theatre once stood, it is thought that it was somewhere beneath what is now Brandon House.

The next location is a small but instantly recognisable building. Further up the hill there is a curved structure made of stone, on the turning to Constitution Hill, with a letterbox built into its frontage. This is Jacob's Well and our next stop.

6. Jacob's Well

The stone building on the junction of Jacob's Well Road and Constitution Hill was probably built sometime in the early 1800s but a building may have stood here since the year 1100.

The structure encloses a naturally occurring hot spring through which water heated deep in the earth's crust was sent bubbling up to the surface. A small chamber was built around it and into it was carved the Hebrew word "zochalim" which means "flowing water." This has led many people to the conclusion that it was likely used as a Jewish cleansing bath called a mikveh or bet tohorah.

Since 1066 the Jewish population of England had been slowly increasing. With the death of Harold II, the more than 500 year rule of the Saxon kings had come to an end and with it came the feudal system. This system created a social hierarchy in which Jews would be tolerated in England and be subjects of the king - however, at the bottom strata of the hierarchy.

It's believed that a small community of Jewish people lived around Brandon Hill in the 12th century, where they were mostly confined to the outskirts of the city. The ritual bath was most likely used as a place for burial ceremonies in which the deceased would be washed in the spring and then bound in a shroud before burial.

By 1290 Edward I enacted the Edict of Expulsion which decreed that every Jewish person should be expelled from the United Kingdom by no later than All Saint's Day of that year. Persecution of Jews had been increasing over the course of the preceding century, with rumours that the Chosen People were at best, greedy and untrustworthy and at worst, hunted and ate children. The edict remained in force until Oliver Cromwell rose to power - and even then was mostly ignored rather than officially retracted.

During the centuries of the Edict of Expulsion, most Jewish buildings were demolished across Britain and Europe. The Jacob's Well, however, was simply covered over and another building constructed on top of it in the 19th century. For this reason, it is believed that it may be the only surviving mikveh of its age anywhere outside of the Holy Land.

The building later became both a small fire station and a bicycle shed for local police officers but it was not until 1987, when a local group of historians excavated the site, that the unique and important relic buried within was discovered.

Keep on climbing up Jacob's Wells Road and take the turning on the left onto Lower Clifton Hill. A little after you have passed the Eldon House pub you will come to a gate on your right through which a small plot of land can be seen along with the remains of a few burial headstones.

7. The Strangers' Burial Ground

An overgrown and eerie plot of land towards the bottom of Lower Clifton Hill is known as the Strangers' Burial Ground.

It was originally built in 1787 to serve as an overflow graveyard for churches in Clifton which were rapidly becoming dense with bodies. Among those buried here was Thomas Beddoes, the physician who pioneered treatments for tuberculosis. Beddoes' body would later be surrounded by countless victims of the disease he had attempted to treat, who had come to Bristol in a last-ditch attempt to find a cure.

During the late 18th century, Hotwells had become a fashionable place for the elite of Britain to visit, with the warm spas along the Avon drawing the wealthy who would spend their days promenading, gossiping, and of course, bathing in the naturally warmed water.

However, Hotwells would become somewhat of a victim of its own success, as the increase in visitors led to an expansion of houses being built and hastily constructed plumbing meant that sewers often leaked into the hot wells. As a result, efforts to improve sanitation enormously increased the cost of visiting Hotwells and soon Georgians returned to holidaying in Bath instead.

By the dawn of the 19th century the spa was still operational but its glory days were behind it. The fashionable elite were leaving the area and were being replaced by a new kind of visitor, who came not for pleasure but out of desperation.

Word had spread that the waters of Hotwells had near miraculous properties and could relieve the symptoms of, and sometimes completely cure, tuberculosis.

Of course, the waters had no such properties and if anything, may have made patients even more infirm as later studies proved that the water had become dangerously polluted. The inevitable often happened and visitors to Hotwells succumbed to their illness and died.

Many of these visitors were buried in the graveyard which came to be known as the Strangers' Burial Ground - an antiquated term for an area of a cemetery where paupers, unclaimed bodies or merely "outsiders" of a town or city were buried. It's not known how many people who died of TB while visiting Hotwells were buried in this plot but sad tales of lives cut tragically short can be found on what few headstones remain.

Continue up Lower Clifton Hill to where it meets Constitution Hill - this stretch is very steep but if you can manage it, the climb is worth it for the views across the city. Head onto Goldney Avenue and take a left, following the wall until you come to the entrance to a rather grand house called Goldney Hall.

8. Goldney Hall

Although it's often closed to the public, it's worth exploring the grounds of the former Goldney House whenever access is permitted, but even from the outside, there's an interesting story to be told of one of Bristol's grandest homes.

The current building serving as Goldney Hall was built in 1724 for Thomas Goldney and his family but was remodelled in the 1860s to sit more fashionably with the rest of Clifton, which had established an architectural look for itself during the Georgian era.

The Goldney family had invested in various seafaring adventures, some of which had ties to the slave trade and privateering (a kind of legalised form of piracy), with Thomas Goldney II the main financial backer of sea captain Woodes Rogers who was involved in the capture of slaves. Rogers would go on to marry the daughter of Thomas Goldney II.

The Goldney family were Quakers and, during the 18th century, they became one of the first religious organisations to openly oppose slavery but it's unclear if the Goldney's went on to play any part in the movement for abolition.

By the 1760s the house was now owned by Thomas Goldney III, who had a flair for the dramatic and romantic, and began redesigning the grounds of the hall into what he hoped would be among the grandest in Clifton.

He set about designing a grotto - a semi-subterranean cave with flowing water - which had become a popular feature of gardens during that era. The grounds also featured a pond with a fountain, which was powered by the garden's most striking feature - an ornate gothic tower.

The tower was built in 1764 and at first appears to be something akin to a folly but actually served as more of a gigantic chimney for a steam engine which could draw water from deep in the ground to the surface, where it would be expelled under pressure to create the fountain and waterfall which flowed through the grotto. This is the first recorded use of a steam engine for this purpose.

Thomas Goldney III died without an heir and the property passed through several owners before being converted into student accommodation in 1956, but the house and much of the fantastical grounds have been preserved - and are well worth a visit if you get a chance.

Continue following the wall until you can see a winding path which leads up the grass embankment on the other side of the road. At the top there is a gate which is topped with an ornate lantern. Go through here, past the war memorial to where the outline of a large building appears on your right as a raised piece of ground with a lawn on top of it.

9. St Andrew's Church

Birdcage Walk is one Clifton's best kept secrets. A secluded avenue of trees which have been trained to form a continuous archway which takes you from Queen's Road to a picturesque little park.

But there are some clues that all is not quite what it seems. An ornate drinking fountain at the Queen's Road end of Birdcage Walk bears the inscription "fear of the LORD is a fountain of life" while at the other is a peculiar area of raised ground which has been manicured into a lawn.

Stranger still, if you peer through the greenery along the walk you will see headstones and tombs on either side, and even an ancient yew tree. You are walking through the grounds of an old churchyard and the raised piece of land was once St Andrew's Church, which was the scene of both devastation and miraculous survival during the Bristol Blitz.

The church was originally built sometime in the 12th century, but as with most of our truly ancient churches, it underwent radical redesign during its existence.

On the evening of the 24th of November, 1940 - an infamous night in Bristol history - the church was hosting evening prayers with a congregation of a few hundred present.

Preparations had been made for the likelihood of a blitz on Bristol, as tensions had mounted across Europe and the threat became even more urgent with the first raid on London on the 7th of September, 1940.

Clifton was a residential area and of no strategic importance, but nevertheless had rehearsed air raid drills and blackouts had been in effect since the outbreak of war. When the sirens went off across the city, the congregation of St Andrew's Church was prepared.

They made their way into the crypts below the church where they could hear the terrifying sound of explosions around the city. The bombs mainly landed around the docks but many residential areas were also hit - and one explosive detonated in the nave of the church, completely obliterating it and leaving only the tower standing.

Miraculously, the congregation was saved, but many people in Clifton and across Bristol lost their lives.

The church tower of St Andrew's remained standing until 1958 when it was demolished and the rest of what remained of the church walls were removed. However, it was decided that the footprint of where the church had stood for centuries should remain and a small park would be built as a memorial to the lives lost throughout the Bristol Blitz and as testament to the fortitude of those who survived it.

Take a stroll through the beautiful Birdcage Walk until you reach Queen's Road. There is a pretty public drinking fountain here, which was installed by Bristol's temperance societies to offer a free alternative to alcohol. Across the street there is a small park called Victoria Square. Cross the road towards it but instead of crossing, head right onto Lansdown Place towards the corner of the park. There is a terrace of Georgian houses and the last one of these features a peculiar engraving close to ground on the side which faces Lansdown Place.

10. Ordnance Survey Benchmarks

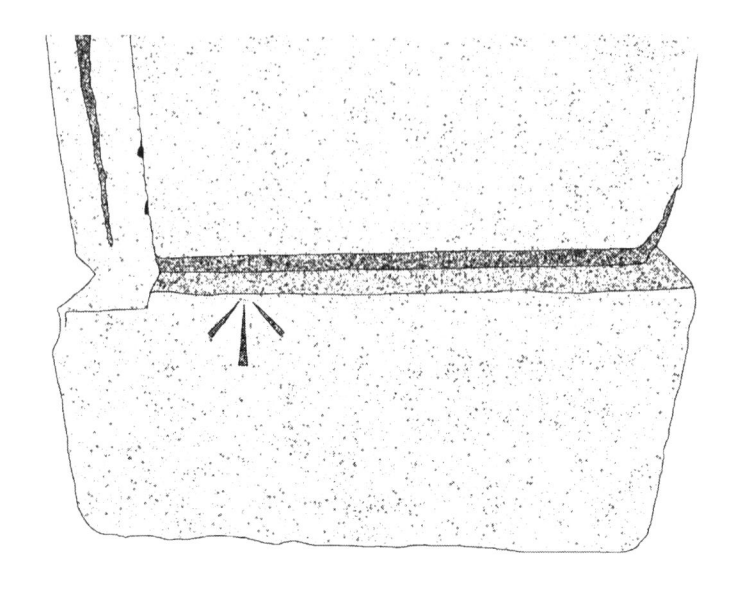

There is nothing uniquely Bristolian about the Ordnance Survey benchmarks you will see etched into buildings across the city (they are usually of an upturned arrow connecting to a horizontal line and normally found close to street level) but I wanted to include them in this book because the city has rather a lot of them - and once you start spotting them you wonder how you ever overlooked them!

Moreover, they are evidence of a bold and brilliant plan which began in the Georgian era and continued until 1993.

Being only a moderately sized island, Britain has been mapped accurately and in great detail for many centuries but the plan for a survey of the entire nation was an innovation, as it would be a means of mapping the landscape in three-dimensions, measuring the topography of the land from all angles - every hill and valley, cliff-face and mountain.

The plan began in 1831, with a few of these markers being carved at points around the country, but it was not fully instigated until 1840 and it was around this time that they were introduced to Bristol.

Using spirit levels (which were placed on a platform which rested in the horizontal crevice of the benchmark) the elevation between two of these marks could be measured (as well as its height above sea level)

Over the course of a century and a half, more and more of these benchmarks were carved and the topographical map of the country became increasingly intricate and precise.

In 1993, the very last of these marks was etched into a pub in the town of Loughton in Essex. Advances in satellite imagery soon afterwards rendered the network of symbols largely irrelevant.

Benchmarks are now a nostalgic reminder of the past and the endeavours of very smart people to thoroughly map the nation. Although they can be found across the country (sometimes in the most surprising places) going on a search for them is just one more way to get out and about exploring our marvellous and fascinating history.

This has been quite a walk! Congratulations if you made is this far. You're on the doorstep of Clifton Village which has countless eateries and pubs to enjoy before making the trek back down the hill!

Walk Nine
Hotwells

Hotwells

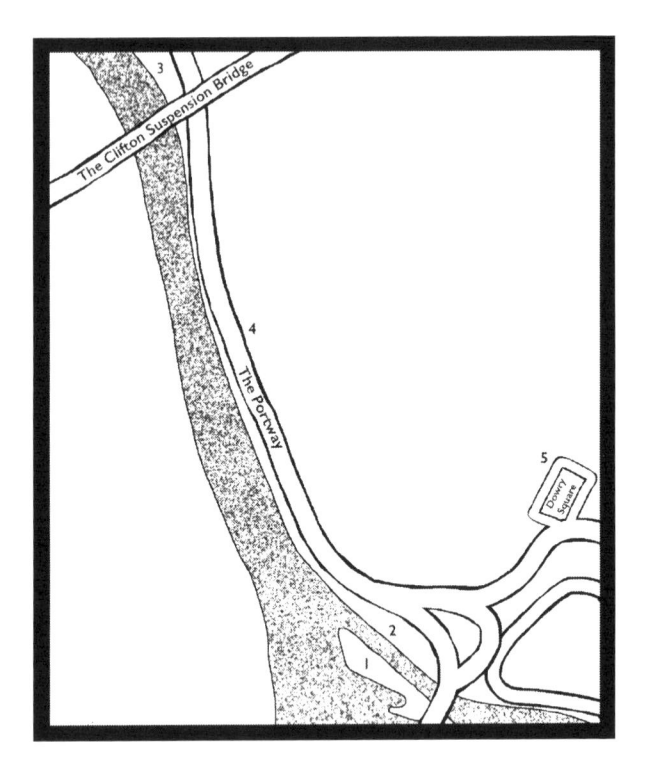

This leisurely stroll along the River Avon will take you through history to the time when the area rivalled Bath as a destination for wealthy Georgians.

Aside from exploring Hotwells' opulent history of promenading and spa bathing, you may be lucky enough to spy what remains of the famous hot spring which gave the area its name. There will also be encounters with a drug addled poet, a legendary crocodile and an explanation for why there's a curious little building on the docks with a precarious lean…

This walk begins at the western edge of Cumberland Basin where it reaches Hotwell Road (under Plimsoll Bridge). On the huge stone jetty which juts out into the Avon there is a small building with a green door which stands at a peculiar angle.

1. The Wonky Building

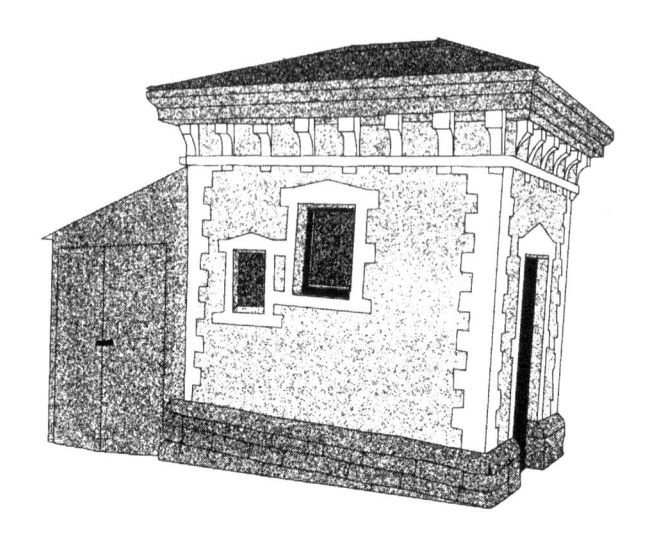

For centuries, Bristol has been at the mercy of the gargantuan tidal range of the River Avon. The Bristol Channel, which feeds into and from the Avon, has the second highest tidal range in the world, after the Bay of Fundy in Canada, and as a result, the river in Bristol can vary from little more than a stream to a 15 metre high surge of water.

The creation of the Floating Harbour in 1809 alleviated a great deal of the flooding the city had been subject to, as the New Cut was capable of diverting enormous amounts of water, but as with all cities built near water, flooding continues to be a risk.

Nowhere is the dramatic power of the tides more apparent than on the "tongue-head" a manmade peninsular of stone between the two docks at the western end of the Floating Harbour, where a little building stands at a crooked angle.

The building is made of pennant stone with attractive detailing around its corners and beneath its roof. It was built around 1887 to serve as a ticket office for the popular Campbell steamers - pleasure boats which would make excursions from Bristol to locations such as Weston-super-Mare and the islands of Steep Holm and Flat Holm.

The ferry steamers would be boarded from the wooden jetties which can be seen along the Hotwells side of the river (they have not aged well and are at constant risk of collapse or demolition) and were still running in parts of the city until 1979. The last of the Campbell fleet of pleasure boats can still be seen in Bristol to this day - the MV Balmoral.

The tongue-head is built high enough out of the water to keep from flooding throughout most of the year, but at exceptionally high tides (usually in the spring and autumn) the Avon can rise high enough to submerge it to a depth of several feet.

This occasional event has been consistent enough that with time the foundations of the ticket office have lost their structural integrity and the tremendous pull of the water has forced the little building to lean at an alarming angle.

Greater flood defences along the New Cut have meant that most of the residential areas of the city have been spared flooding for many decades, but as sea levels around the world continue to rise, it is of vital importance that Bristol adapts to our rapidly changing planet if it is to survive into the future.

From this spot there is more than just the old ticket office and the tongue-head to be seen. The next stop on this walk takes place right where you are, as it is the very place where the first ever image of the legendary Bristol Crocodile was taken!

2. The Bristol Crocodile

In 2014 a sensational story swept across Bristol when a bus driver spotted something strange in the New Cut. A crocodile.

A wet, grey winter had swamped Bristol and the people of the city were enthralled by this bizarre and novel story as a distraction from the gloomy days. Could there really be a crocodile in Bristol's waterways?

The short answer was almost certainly not. According to experts on the creatures, the Avon and Frome were far too cold in the early months of the year to support an animal used to living in tropical heat and their natural food supplies were not found in the abundance they would need to survive, but this did not stop further stories of the mystery croc arising.

The initial report would probably have vanished without a trace had it not been for a post on Twitter from Avon and Somerset police chief Nick Gargan, which revealed not just the sighting, but that police would be investigating. For whatever reason, the story caught the imagination of Bristolians and the rest of the country alike.

Despite claims that the croc could simply not survive a British winter, two days after the initial sighting a book-keeper driving by Coronation Bridge claimed to have witnessed the elusive beast and that the shock nearly caused her to crash her car.

In response, Bristol Zoo, Noah's Ark Zoo Farm and Bristol Aquarium confirmed that all of their animals had been accounted for and a production company which was filming a horror film about a man-eating alligator on the Somerset levels released a statement denying that they were responsible or had arranged a publicity stunt.

Following a report of two crocodiles in Eastville Park, police in riot gear descended on the area but found no trace of either creature. Soon afterwards, the crocodile was making headlines across the world.

After at least four sightings of the creature, which had now been dubbed Cristol, (a portmanteau of crocodile and Bristol) seemed to vanish until June of 2014 when a jogger snapped a photograph of it in the River Avon at Hotwells.

The photograph was not the last to be taken of Cristol, as soon she was posing for pictures and videos throughout Bristol (often looking remarkably similar to a log floating in the water) and while many newspaper stories tried to claim that Bristol was either "gripped by fear" or imply that the city was made up of parochial simpletons for believing this nonsense, in truth, most Bristolians reacted to the story as a goofy bit of fun.

Pubs along the waterways put up signs saying "No Crocs Allowed" and tongue-in-cheek warnings were posted around the harbour, alerting people of the beast and her ferocious appetite. Years after the first sightings, Cristol was memorialised in a crocheted life-sized replica which was made by dozens of volunteers.

Reports of the crocodile continued throughout 2014 and the following year, but never at the rate they had initially. By 2017 sightings seemed to dry up altogether and most people forgot that Cristol had ever been a sensation. That was until August of that year, when an engineer at Chew Valley Lake made a remarkable discovery.

Walking along the edge of the reservoir which serves as Bristol's water supply was a baby caiman - a reptile very similar to an alligator or crocodile. The creature measured a little over half a foot long but the species was capable of growing up to fifteen feet.

The caiman was caught and handed over to the RSPCA and was later re-homed at Crocodiles of the World zoo in Oxfordshire. No explanation for its appearance at the lake was ever found.

Most people believe that Cristol was little more than logs floating through Bristol's murky waterways combined with a touch of media sensationalising. The winter of 2013/2014 had been an unusually wet one and the rivers had brought a great deal of detritus towards the city, but with the discovery of the caiman, the people of the city paused to ponder the unthinkable.

Could Cristol actually have been real after all?

We're leaving the harbour behind and heading west. If the tide is low it's worth seeing if you can spot Bristol's very own hot spring - the naturally warmed water which gave Hotwells its name. Follow the Avon past the tumbledown jetties and under the Clifton Suspension Bridge until you come to the intersection of the Portway and Bridge Valley Road

If the tide is high the spring is impossible to see. In which case, follow the Avon until you reach the Colonnade on the right, which is a crescent of redbrick houses. Unfortunately you'll have to just imagine the spring for the following stop!

3. The Hot Well

At low tides along the mudbanks of the Avon it is sometimes possible to spot thin streams of water gurgling up through the silt. They can break through at several points along the river but can most usually be spotted near to where the Portway and Bridge Valley Road meet.

Unfortunately it's a rather disappointing dribble nowadays and it can be hard to imagine why it was worth making such a fuss about, but historically it was much more impressive.

It has been constantly flowing into Bristol since at least the 15th century and was a popular bathing spot throughout the Tudor era, at which time it was coloured a greyish white and probably had a lightly sulphurous smell akin to rotten eggs.

The source of the spring is the same as the one which feeds the Roman Baths in Bath - the Mendip Hills, but it does not flow with as much force nor as much heat. The water which emerges from beneath the ground is believed to have fallen as rain onto the Mendips thousands of years ago, where it sank beneath the earth to a tremendous depth into cracks in the earth's crust, before being superheated and forced upwards through a network of underground tunnels before emerging in both Bristol and Bath.

The reason why Bristol's spring water is notably cooler is because it flows closer to the surface on route to the Avon, and therefore is mixed with more groundwater.

Even though the spring may not be as impressive as the one gushing into Bath, it is still a remarkable thought that the water that can be seen emerging constantly in

Bristol has been underground for millennia and has only at this very moment broken through to the surface.

If you walked to the intersection of the Portway and Bridge Valley Road, head back to the Colonnade.

4. The Colonnade

It can be hard to imagine what the stretch of land running parallel to the River Avon once looked like, as the Portway dominates the area. When the road was completed in 1926 it was the most expensive road ever built in Britain, costing over £45 million in today's money, and completely changed the look and feel of Hotwells.

In its heyday, towards the end of the 18th century, Hotwells would have been abuzz with visitors promenading along the riverfront. Promenading was a popular pastime among the elite of Georgian Britain and involved wandering up and down a street in your most fashionable attire. Men and women would often do this arm in arm, nodding at other couples as they passed and inspecting each others' clothes.

Sometimes couples would swap partners and often women would promenade together to exchange gossip. Young bachelors too would promenade in pairs and the whole process would be played out over hours and hours.

Another of the most popular pastimes of the day was geology and the collecting of gemstones. Visitors to Hotwells would often spend their days searching the gorge for Bristol Diamonds - a type of quartz crystal found only in the Avon Gorge.

Business people were quick to capitalise on this influx of wealthy visitors to the area. In 1786 the Colonnade, the delightful crescent terrace of buildings on the Portway, was opened. It is now a row of houses but when it was built it was actually a shopping arcade of fashionable boutiques with the latest and finest garments from London on display in its windows, along with quaint eateries and bijou jewellers.

The idea of a shopping arcade was not unique, but the idea of a purpose-built complex to cater for tourists was a first for Bristol. Unfortunately its popularity was only temporary.

The Colonnade is the sole remaining structure from the complex of buildings which once lined the river, the most notable of which was the pump room, which drew warm water from the hot spring into a bathing spa. Another spa was built in Clifton.

Hotwells never achieved the same popularity as Bath and its draw as a tourist destination was short-lived. During the 19th century there were a couple of attempts to relaunch the area as an alternative to Bath but neither of these were successful and eventually the glory days of Hotwells faded into the past.

The Colonnade may be the last of the buildings remaining from that era, but we do have one other remnant of Georgian Hotwells which will likely remain even more permanent. In 1791 a young J. M. W. Turner travelled to Bristol and a collection of his sketches and paintings capture the beauty of the area as it once was. The most famous of these is *The Avon Gorge and Bristol Hotwell*, which features not just the old pump house but the lovely and familiar crescent of the Colonnade.

There is a fair bit of backtracking to do to get to our next location, but it's well worth it as there's a fascinating story to be found. Follow the Portway back towards the harbour and when it splits into three roads, take the one which veers left and follow Hotwell Road around the corner. When you are level with a red telephone box you have reached Dowry Square. Look for the houses numbered six and seven.

5. Thomas Beddoes

Thomas Beddoes was born in Shropshire in 1760 but thanks to his pioneering work in medicine, he will always be linked to Bristol.

In 1799, he opened the Pneumatic Institution, a medical research facility at the site of what is now number six and seven, Dowry Square and it was there that his attempts to cure tuberculosis became tied to his primary scientific interest - that of nitrous oxide - laughing gas.

Beddoes had a fascination with the treatment of diseases and had received a degree in medicine at the University of Edinburgh. He had a particular urge to address the common but often fatal disease of tuberculosis, so shortly after graduating in 1786, he moved to Bristol where a huge number of sufferers could be found, as they had come to the city in hopes that the Hotwells spa would cure them.

The Pneumatic Institution was not Beddoes first medical facility in the city. He opened a clinic in Hope Square in Hotwells in 1793 and began using patients to test his theories on the inhalation of gases as a possible cure for their ailments.

This took a most extraordinary form. For a long time it had been noted that butchers were infected by tuberculosis at rates far lower than the rest of the population, but nobody could work out why this might be.

Beddoes theory was that cows were giving off some sort of gas which made the butchers immune. As a result, he kept a small herd of cows on Hope Square which he would have breathe over sickly patients. While this may now seem rather bizarre, Edward Jenner developed his smallpox vaccine in 1793 after noticing that milkmaids very rarely developed the disease - and his inoculation was itself derived from cows.

His clinic on Hope Square was soon too small to accommodate the number of patients and to perform his necessary experiments, so he opened his Pneumatic Institution in 1799. By this time, Beddoes had become fascinated by the properties of laughing gas and most of his treatments were based on a presumption that the gas must be performing some kind of positive function.

One of his colleagues at this time was Humphrey Davy, the chemist who is probably best known for inventing the Davy lamp, which could provide a safe source of light in areas containing flammable gas - an invention which saved the lives of countless miners.

However, it was the institution's most regular client for which it's now best remembered - Samuel Taylor Coleridge. Coleridge was a poet who wrote *The Rime of the Ancient Mariner* and *Kubla Khan* among many other works. Unfortunately he is not read as often as he probably should be, most likely because the Romantic Movement is currently going through a period of unpopularity, but hopefully the future will see a revival of interest.

Aside from being a poet, Coleridge was a notorious addict - addicted to pretty much every substance it was possible to get addicted to. He was friends with Thomas Beddoes and his interest in nitrous oxide was a far less honourable one. Very soon, Coleridge had added laughing gas to the long list of substances he was dependent on.

The Pneumatic Institution lasted only two short years. A typhus infection had spread across Bristol and it was decided that the best way to deal with the spread of the disease was to convert the institution into a more traditional hospital.

Beddoes died in 1808 at the age of 48. He left behind a complicated legacy, with many claiming that his career was essentially a series of failures. However, in more recent years there has been a reappraisal of his work and it is often said that Beddoes true revolutionary idea was in establishing dedicated research institutes in Hope Square and Dowry Square - a tradition which continues to this day.

That is the end of this walk. I recommend a pleasant stroll along the harbourside or a snack at the nearby Pickle Cafe at Underfall Yard.

Walk Ten
Arnos Vale Cemetery

Arnos Vale Cemetery

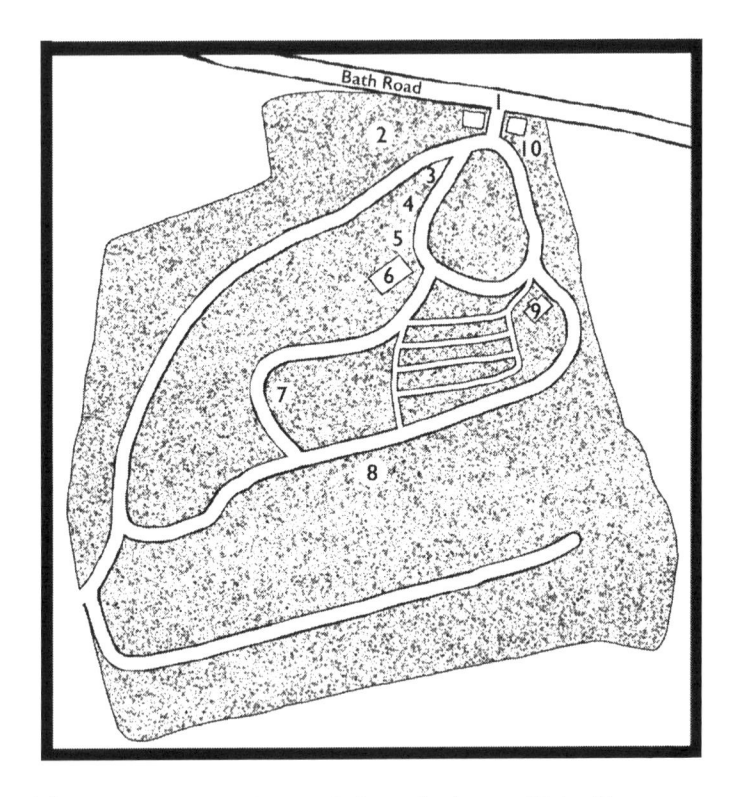

There are cemeteries and there is Arnos Vale Cemetery. A sprawling, achingly gothic masterpiece which is the eternal home of over 300,000 former residents of Bristol.

As I'm sure you can imagine, this walk explores some rather dark topics, not least of all the inevitability of death and is therefore not suitable for everyone. It is also a rather tricky walk in places, with uneven paths and steep climbs.

However, for those who are willing and able to join me for an exploration of our most fascinating burial ground, I can promise you stories of ghosts, bats and premature burial but also a much loved preacher, a wartime hero and a pair of revolutionary thinkers who helped change the world…

This walk begins at the Bath Road entrance to Arnos Vale Cemetery. The cemetery is open from 9am to 5pm every day. The chapels are open from 10am to 4pm.

1. The Necropolis

Bristol can boast an array of beautiful and historic burial grounds but Arnos Vale Cemetery is indisputably the queen of them all. It's not just a tranquil, contemplative place to while away the hours but also a wildlife haven amidst Bristol's urban sprawl.

The plot of land on which the cemetery now sits was purchased in 1837 and the beautiful buildings that can be found among the gravestones and tombs were designed by Bristol-based architect Charles Underwood, who took inspiration from ancient Greece in creating the chapels and gatehouses.

Arnos Vale was intended to be more than just a cemetery, it was to be a necropolis - literally meaning "city of the dead" - an ornate, vast and beautiful burial ground that the wealthiest and most fashionable residents of Bristol would literally be dying to get into.

Evergreen plants were planted throughout - selected to subtly hint at the idea of life being everlasting, and among them can be found trees from around the world, including Himalayan cedars and Chilean pines.

The first person to be buried in Arnos Vale Cemetery was Mary Breillart. She was laid to rest on the 29th of July, 1839 and her obelisk-style tombstone was given a plot which would have overlooked the entire city. Over the course of the following 180 years trees have grown through what was once open fields, obscuring the view but creating a shady, tranquil woodland to replace it.

Mary Breillart was not alone for long and soon she had many neighbours. The open and unblemished landscape of Arnos Vale made it an attractive option for those wealthy enough to be buried there, especially when compared to the overcrowded urban cemeteries which were perpetually shrouded beneath Bristol's smoggy skies and often darkened by layers of industrial soot.

To walk among the graves of Arnos Vale Cemetery is a tour of Victorian burial fashion. Most of the gravestones were simple and classic in design but others were more daring. Some of the earliest burials feature Egyptian inspired tombstones - relics from an age when Victorian England went crazy for Egyptology, while others are more stark and timeless - a personal favourite of mine being a gigantic boulder of rugged rock.

During the 20th century, Arnos Vale became somewhat neglected and the once pristine landscape was soon claimed by nature. For many decades it became something of an oddity - an overgrown woodland with gravestones poking through shrubbery, but thanks to tireless efforts from volunteers and charitable grants from several organisations, the cemetery has been restored in a beautiful fashion.

Although the area you encounter when you first enter through the gates is gorgeously manicured, the woodland which had grown through the tombstones elsewhere was allowed to thrive and become an important oasis for many of our local species.

Nowadays, the cemetery has become more than a place just to memorialise the dead, you can take pilates classes among the gravestones, watch films projected onto the side of the chapels, experience open-air plays and poetry readings or just enjoy a cup of coffee in the cafe.

Head through the gates and turn right. You will be able to see the Great War Memorial, which is perched on a low hill above the cemetery. Follow the path and look for the gravestone of Harry Blanshard Wood.

2. Harry Blanshard Wood

A quiet hill in Arnos Vale Cemetery, Soldier's Corner is the solemn and dignified final resting place for 530 servicemen and women who died in the First and Second World Wars.

There are countless stories to tell of lives cut tragically short among these victims of war, but that of Harry Blanshard Wood is certainly one of the most remarkable - as he was one of only 627 men awarded the Victoria Cross for their actions during WWI.

The Victoria Cross is the highest honour that can be awarded to soldiers for acts of extreme valour and bravery in the face of the enemy.

Wood was born in Newton on Derwent, Yorkshire in 1882. He enlisted with the army at a young age and worked his way up to the rank of corporal. When war broke out across Europe Harry was aged 32 and served with the 2nd Battalion Scots Guard of the British Army.

While fighting in the trenches Wood became lost in No-Mans-Land and stumbled into enemy territory, attracting a group of Germans. Wood was able to shoot two of them and took a third hostage before fleeing. For his quick thinking he was later presented with the Award of Military Medal.

However, it was for his actions on the 13th of October, 1918 that he was awarded the Victoria Cross. In the village of St Python, France, Wood's platoon came under fire and his sergeant was struck and killed, meaning that Wood, as corporal, was instantly in charge of his men.

Acting quickly, and presumably with the kind of strength reported by people in times of immense stress,

Wood seized a huge rock and hauled it into the middle of a street which was being raked by gunfire.

From behind the rock Wood was able to cover his men as they fled to a bridge across the River Selle. All the men in his platoon made it to safety and Wood escaped unharmed.

Despite being awarded the prestigious honour, Harry Blanchard Wood had been scarred by war in ways that were not immediately apparent. Nowadays we have a better understanding of the extreme anguish that is caused by post traumatic stress disorder but the prevailing attitude of the time was that men should keep their feelings to themselves.

In 1924, Harry Wood was on holiday with his wife in Teignmouth, Devon. A car accidentally mounted the pavement and struck Harry's wife, who was walking beside him. She received only a minor injury, but he collapsed on the spot and fell into a coma from which he never recovered.

It was a tragic end to a heroic man's life. He was only 42.

He was buried in a prime location in Soldier's Corner as a mark of respect for his actions in the theatre of war. In 2018 - 100 years to the day since he was awarded the Victoria Cross, Harry Blanchard Wood was given a permanent memorial in the Yorkshire village of Newton on Derwent, where he was born.

A representative of Wood's family said at the unveiling of the memorial "The act of war brings out the best and worst in a man, in circumstances many of us cannot imagine. In Harry it brought out the best qualities a man can possess. He was a true hero."

Head back down the hill towards the entrance. When the path splits to the right you will see a marble obelisk. This is the grave of Reverend John Adey Pratt and is the next stop on this walk.

3. The Penny Memorial

One of the most striking and easily recognisable monuments in Arnos Vale Cemetery is the handsome, marble obelisk dedicated to the Reverend John Adey Pratt, or as he was more affectionately known, "The Children's Preacher".

The most noticeable feature of the tomb is the charming depiction of Rev. Pratt himself, seated before a small group of children and presumably preaching, while a beam of divine light shines upon them. Exposure to the elements has worn most of the faces smooth but enough of it remains to make it clear that this was a man who was remembered very fondly after his death.

Not much is known about John Pratt's early life but he was born in October of 1811 and did not appear to have aspirations as a holy man until shortly after his 20th birthday. He was living in London and claimed to have experienced a religious encounter from which he concluded he was being called into service on behalf of the Lord.

It was at this time that he began visiting workhouses, hospitals and even prisons to provide sermons. He would even preach to navvies - the mostly Irish workers who were digging canals across the country - who were regarded by much of society as semi-feral drunks who were beneath even the salvation of Christ.

In 1850, the independent chapel of St. Phillips in Bristol had lost its reverend and was hoping to employ a Protestant minister in a permanent role. Pratt was invited to preach at the church and unbeknown to him, many of the congregation were regarding this as an audition.

His service was extremely well received and the congregation, which was run on largely egalitarian grounds, was allowed to choose themselves who their preacher would be. Pratt was offered the position and accepted. He moved to Bristol immediately.

Reverend Pratt was well liked by all his congregation but the children of his parish were particularly fond of him. Often described as being almost childlike in character himself, the preacher had an optimistic and playful way of bringing Bible stories to life and was an enormously engaging speaker at Sunday schools. For this reason he was given the nickname "The Children's Preacher".

Throughout his life he was described as being concerned with all aspects of the struggles working class people encountered and continued to give sermons to the poorer people of the city right up until his sudden death in 1867.

His unexpected demise was a tremendous shock not just to his congregation but to the children who had been so fond of him. A city wide effort to raise funds for a suitably impressive memorial resulted in a huge donation of £400 by Henry Overton Wills II of the Wills Tobacco Company (who was a Nonconformist and friend of Reverend Pratt) while a further £100 was raised by Sunday school children in Bristol.

It is believed (or at least rumoured) that the children raised this money by each of them bringing a single penny to Sunday school. Whether this story is true is unclear, but it hasn't stopped the glorious monument to Reverend Pratt in Arnos Vale Cemetery being dubbed "The Penny Memorial".

The next stop is mere feet away. The unmissable and grandiose tomb to Raja Ram Mohan Roy.

4. Ram Mohan Roy

Easily the most photographed monument in Arnos Vale Cemetery is the tomb of Ram Mohan Roy. He is often regarded as one of the most significant figures in Indian history, so it may seem rather peculiar that a man who is often regarded as "the father of modern India" would come to be buried in a cemetery in Bristol.

Ram Mohan Roy was born in 1772 in Radhanagar, India, which was then under British rule. During his education he was exposed to teachings from Persian and Arabic cultures, which first started his questioning of many of the traditions and customs of the Hindu faith which he had been born into - most significantly that of polytheism - the belief in more than one god.

Shortly after learning how to speak English, Ram Mohan Roy showed an interest in Unitarianism and co-founded a society in Calcutta. He began campaigning against many of the practices in Indian society which he found abhorrent, most notably the tradition of *sati,* where a widow was expected to climb atop her deceased husband's funeral pyre and be burned alongside him.

He also campaigned against child brides, polygamy and the dowry system of exchanging daughters for material goods in wedding arrangements. These campaigns earned Ram Mohan Roy many enemies but he won many more supporters.

After exposing how much revenue was being taken out of India and sent directly to England (about half of the nation's entire earnings per year), he became something of an arbiter between the two countries, appealing for a more just treatment of Indian people, and in 1830, he travelled to England to meet members of Parliament in a successful appeal for a fairer deal on behalf of his nation.

While visiting Bristol in 1833, Ram Mohan Roy suddenly took ill and died shortly afterwards on the 27th of September. The cause of death was believed to be meningitis. He was 61 years old.

He was buried in Stapleton but almost immediately there were calls for him to have a more prestigious burial, reflecting his great importance to the people of India. In 1843 his body was exhumed and he was buried beneath a simple tomb in Arnos Vale. The ornate structure built over the top was added a few years later and is based on traditional Indian *chhatri* - an architectural feature which literally translates as "umbrella".

In a further mark of respect for the great Indian reformer, a statue of Raja Ram Mohan Roy was unveiled in 1997. Cast in bronze by sculptor Niranjan Pradham, the statue can be found outside the Bristol Central Library.

Keep following the path away from the entrance towards a large building in front of you. It is now known as the Spielman Centre but was originally a Nonconformist chapel. It is the next stop on this walk.

5. The Chapels

Aside from being a place of eternal rest, Arnos Vale was also built as a business venture and investors wanted to maximise their profits by ensuring that as many Bristolians as possible would want to be buried in the city's most prestigious cemetery.

The burial ground is now home to about 300,000 corpses - equivalent to around two-thirds of Bristol's living population. One of the reasons for its success as a cemetery is probably due to the presence of two chapels, one for Anglican funeral services and one for Nonconformist burials.

The term "Nonconformist" actually refers to several branches of Protestant Christianity who sit outside the doctrines of Anglicanism. Among them are Calvinists, Congregationalists and Presbyterians but often refers to Methodists, Unitarians and Quakers too, who have had a long association with Bristol.

Throughout much of British history, Nonconformists have experienced degrees of discrimination, the most alarming of which was during the reign of "Bloody" Mary, when several hundred were burned to death. As alternative forms of Christianity took hold across the country, so too did the amount to which they were tolerated, although the universities of Oxford, Cambridge and Durham only permitted Nonconformists (as well as Catholics and non-Christians) in 1871.

By the 1850s it was estimated that as many as half of those regularly attending church services in England identified as part of a Nonconformist denomination, so it's likely that the Nonconformist chapel (and its surrounding burial grounds) would have been almost as popular as the Anglican chapel (the other large building that can be found in the cemetery) when they were opened within Arnos Vale in 1839.

The Nonconformist chapel now serves as an exhibition centre as well as a cafe, but the main hall of the building remains a quiet space that has been tastefully restored and serves as a reminder of all those members of our society who have fallen outside of traditional Anglican thinking.

The next stop on this walk is rather a dark and potentially upsetting one, as it deals with the process of cremation and features the actual equipment used in the practice. If you are interested in seeing the crematorium, it can be found on the lower floor beneath the cafe. Turn right before the toilets and you will be guided through to the furnace.

If you don't want to visit the crematorium, you can either read the next section from where you are - or alternatively, you can skip it all together!

6. The Crematorium

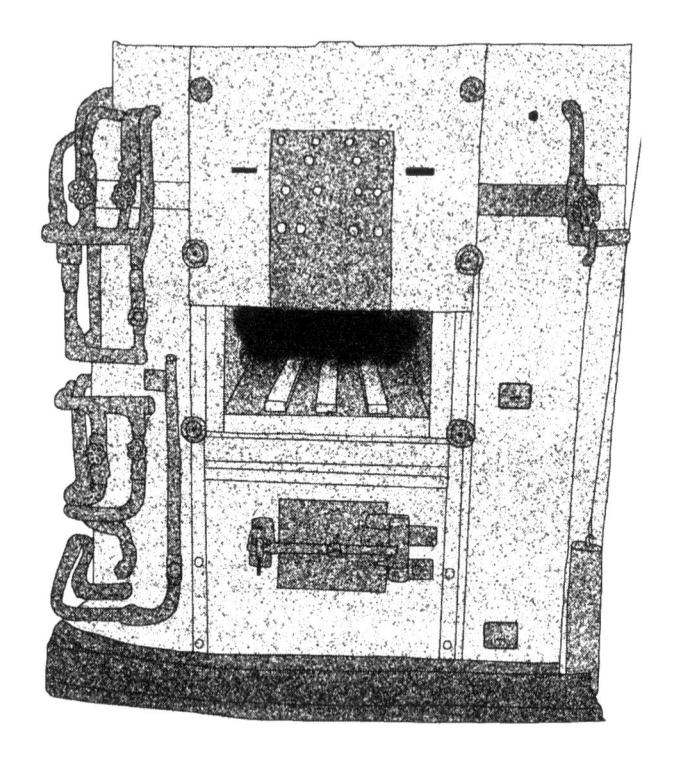

Beneath the Spielman Centre in Arnos Vale Cemetery there is a stark and haunting contraption. It is a furnace and was used to incinerate countless bodies.

I have always believed that one of the best aspects of visiting burial grounds, particularly historic ones, is not just to enjoy the overgrown beauty of places which have often been left for nature to claim, but to attempt to confront something that few of us feel comfortable doing - the inevitability of death - and there are few places where that confrontation feels more acute than in the Arnos Vale Crematorium.

The furnace and the surrounding crematorium were built from 1928-1929 and proved such a popular alternative to burials that others were added to the cemetery soon afterwards. By the 1950s, it had become such a booming industry that Arnos Vale would host up to thirty cremations a day, with each individual furnace being capable of incinerating seven bodies from dawn until dusk.

To speed up this process, a platform was installed in the roof of the crematorium, which can still be seen today. Services would be held in the chapel above and then a curtain would be drawn around the casket which was then lowered through the floor.

Cremations would often take several hours and with a backlog of bodies piling up on busy days, a cremulator was installed to help speed up the process. A cremulator is a device used to grind up the bone fragments found in ash deposited by the furnaces (often referred to as "cremains") and the variety found in Arnos Vale is believed to be the only one of its kind on public display in Britain.

It operated almost like a marble run, with cremains rolling down slopes and through grinders until a thin, ash-like powder poured from the bottom which could then be scattered either in a dedicated section of the cemetery or at a location chosen by friends and family (a practice which is technically illegal without permission but is generally tolerated as long as it is done discretely.)

Cremation is known to have been carried out in ancient, pre-Christian England but its association with Pagan religions is thought to be why early Christian settlers put a stop to it. There was also a belief among some denominations that on Judgement Day, the dead would literally be resurrected in bodily form and must therefore go into the ground as intact as possible.

By the Victorian era, cemeteries across the land were chock full with corpses and our small island was running out of locations to bury our dead. The Victorians also had a rather ghoulish preoccupation with being buried alive and so calls were soon being made publicly for cremation to be decriminalised.

In 1874, the Cremation Society was founded and by 1878 they had built their first working crematorium in which they successfully incinerated the body of a horse. Despite their best efforts to get the law overturned, it was not until 1902 that a bill was passed through parliament which legalised cremation.

The practice remained somewhat taboo throughout the early years of the 20th century but following the outbreak of WWI, and the devastating loss of life it resulted in, attitudes towards death and burial changed drastically. By the turn of the 21st century, over 75% of funerals were cremations.

Arnos Vale crematorium offers a rare opportunity to see a furnace, and it is a sobering sight. Often the practices involved in death are hidden from view, but those who want a peek behind the curtains - and perhaps even a glimpse at their own fates, it's a powerful and important experience.

We are returning above ground. Retrace your steps until you are outside and head towards the Garden of Rest, which is situated beside the Spielman Centre. Here the cremains of 69 servicemen and women from WWII were laid to rest in a beautiful remembrance garden. On the path which leads from the memorial, take the third turning on the left, which will lead uphill through a woodland. There is a crook in the path which marks roughly where the halfway point of the hill is and a little walk on from here you should be able to find an attractive but simple gravestone of a cross. This is the grave of Mary Carpenter.

7. Mary Carpenter

Resting beneath a plain but attractive headstone in a shady, woodland corner of Arnos Vale Cemetery are all that was mortal of one of Bristol's greatest citizens. Mary Carpenter.

Carpenter was born in Exeter in 1807 and was the eldest child of Lant Carpenter, a Unitarian minister. When she was ten years old, her father was offered a job at a church near Lewin's Mead in Bristol and she and her family moved to the city.

Mary became engaged in many social issues from a young age. Unitarianism has often been a home for radicals and progressive values and it's believed that her father's association with the church likely brought her into contact with some fairly revolutionary ideas.

She had a particular interest in the education of the poor and the reform of prisons, and her early campaigns brought her to the attention of Raja Ram Mohan Roy (who was the subject of an earlier stop on this walk and who is also buried in Arnos Vale Cemetery) and it is through him she became associated with the plight of the poor, and especially poor women in India.

By the 1850s, Carpenter was writing extensively on the horrendous conditions the working class of Victorian England were suffering, as well as the need for reform of prisoners from underprivileged backgrounds. Some of these writings were so radical that they were condemned by Pope Pius IX in the 1860s.

She was a woman of deeds as well as words and in 1852 she established a reformatory school to educate poor children in the Kingswood area of Bristol. This was followed by another school in what is now the Red Lodge Museum on Park Row and is believed to be the first school of its kind anywhere in the world established to educate girls who had grown up among poverty and crime.

In the 1860s she travelled to India and witnessed firsthand the dire need for education among women and girls and went on to co-found, and fund, several schools on the subcontinent for the rest of her life.

Mary Carpenter died in her sleep at the Red Lodge in 1877. Her passing was felt acutely across Bristol and her funeral cortège to Arnos Vale Cemetery was attended by thousands of admirers and stretched for over half a mile.

She is now remembered not just as one of the greatest social reformers of the 19th century, but one of the most remarkable people ever to have lived in Bristol.

Continue up the path to the top of the hill and then take a left and head downwards. You should soon be able to see an obelisk-style tomb belonging to Mary Breillart. This will be the next stop on this walk.

8. The Ghosts of Arnos Vale

A cemetery may seem the sort of location you might expect to be teeming with ghosts, but according to English folklore, most graveyards have only one spirit - a guardian or protector of the area who is usually the first person ever to be interred in the burial ground.

If that were the case, Mary Breillart, who was the first person to be buried in Arnos Vale Cemetery in 1839, could be expected to be filling such a role but there are no recorded sightings of Mary at all. That's not to say that the burial ground is without ghosts, according to popular legend, at least two restless spirits have regularly been sighted.

One of these is sometimes referred to as "the widow" and is only ever seen at the Soldiers' Corner area of the cemetery. Wearing grey and often weeping on her knees, it has led some people to assume that she is the widow of a fallen soldier who is buried somewhere beneath the memorial.

The weeping widow is not always seen as much as she is felt. Visitors to the cemetery claim to have felt a sudden, unexpected chill accompanied by an intense sensation of overwhelming sadness.

Another ghost said to haunt the cemetery has usually been spotted in the overgrown woodland that has taken over much of Arnos Vale. Her appearance is often preceded by a bloodcurdling scream, followed by her manifestation as a panicked woman in torn burial clothes.

Some have speculated that the woman could have been the victim of a premature burial sometime in the Victorian era and had been mistaken for dead after suffering a sickness which gave her the appearance of a corpse. Later she woke in her grave and died trying to scream for help.

As disturbing a story as it may be, it's highly unlikely that anybody was ever buried alive at Arnos Vale Cemetery. By the time the gates were opened in 1839, advances in medical practices as well as an increase in the amount of time it took to arrange a funeral, it would have been unlikely anyone in England would have been accidentally buried alive.

Whether or not you believe in ghosts, the stories we tell about supposedly haunted places may say as much about our own fears of death as they do about the spirits themselves. In a place built to house the dead, it's little wonder that minds have a habit of wandering and perhaps even creating phantoms hiding in the shadows.

Continue down the path towards the other chapel in the grounds. Looking at the glorious chapel from the front, there will be a subterranean entrance to crypts found on the left side of the building. This is quite a dark and quiet place and there's also some commentary from me on the grisly process of human decomposition, so it might only be suited for those who enjoy a touch of the macabre…

9. The Crypt

Beneath the Anglican chapel in Arnos Vale Cemetery there is rather eerie little space. Damp and perpetually gloomy, even on bright summer days, the crypt was actually built as the more attractive alternative to traditional burial when the cemetery first opened.

The Anglican chapel itself is easily the most impressive building in the grounds. While the Nonconformist chapel was kept relatively simple in design, architect Charles Underwood created an imposing Neoclassical monument to be the central feature of the original cemetery's layout and as such was meant to be suitably breathtaking.

The crypts were intended to be a small, elite space for bodies to be interred in vaults above the ground. Corpses would be laid in lead coffins and slid into deep spaces within the walls with a memorial plaque, sealing them away forever.

The reasons for wanting to be put to eternal rest in this way were many. Throughout the Georgian and Victorian era, fear of live burial was acute. Following outbreaks of typhus and cholera, great swathes of the country had died within weeks of each other and this led to rumours that not everyone who had been buried had actually died.

While these rumours were largely unfounded, cemetery operators were quick to capitalise on them and inventions such as underground breathing tubes and pulley systems that would ring an above ground bell were patented and installed in graves across the country. There was at least a chance, if you were buried in an over ground crypt, that somebody might hear you screaming for rescue.

Another reason was a fear of decay, which remains one of the primary reasons why people opt for cremations in such great numbers nowadays. For many, the idea of eventually turning to mush and being eaten by worms was such an unsettling concept that they would prefer any alternative.

Of course, even a lead-lined coffin could only preserve a body for so long. Even in a hermetically sealed tomb, a body will bloat from the bacteria inside it and may even burst - which caused many vaults to leak and even rupture with time. For some, however, this was still preferable to an underground burial.

The third, and probably most common reason for a crypt burial, was simply one of status. Space was limited in the crypt and therefore it was the most expensive to be interred in. Kings, saints and prophets had long been left to their endless sleep in above-ground monuments, so the practice had an air of tremendous importance about it and it was expected that the eternal residents of the crypt would be made up of only the wealthiest and most important figures in Bristol society of the time.

This was not to be the case. Only a little over thirty bodies were ever interred in the crypt and most of the vaults were never used. For whatever reason, the chamber never appealed to the public in the way its designer had hoped and now it remains a quiet, yet somewhat eerie, relic of the past

Go back outside and follow the path towards the main entrance to the cemetery. There are a couple of stone lodges here which now serve as a visitor centre and gift shop. This will be the last stop on this walk.

10. The Arnos Vale Bats

Standing proud at either side of the entrance gate to Arnos Vale Cemetery are two handsome, neoclassical lodges made from Bath stone, appearing much like miniature versions of the Parthenon in Athens. The lodges were once houses for the cemetery staff and their families.

Although they may at first glance look rather small homes for multiple families to have lived, once inside you will find that they are surprisingly deep and airy, and in a time when working class families were expected to live in fairly confined spaces, these two buildings were probably quite a tempting offer to many lower income workers.

The lodges are actually joined together by a tunnel which runs beneath the entrance. This was so that people could freely pass from one building to the other without causing any kind of disturbance if a funeral was taking place.

Although the lodges are no longer home to anyone, this underground passage has become a roost for one of the country's most important species - bats. At least four species of native bat are known to live in the tunnel between the lodges and admittance to see them is strictly prohibited except for rare occasions.

Britain's bat population is among the most protected species in the world. So vital is the role that they play in nature that these wild animals have more legal protection than domestic pets.

Aside from acting as a kind of natural pesticide, by keeping insect populations from getting out of control, bats are also a bellwether animal - the health of an ecosystem can be measured by the abundance of its bat population.

Arnos Vale Cemetery is a Site of Nature Conservation Interest, meaning that its plan to manage the landscape is done in a way which is sympathetic to local flora and fauna. If you spend any time in this wonderful cemetery keep an eye open for birds, butterflies, occasional deer, wildflowers and of course, those charming and precious bats.

Arnos Vale Cemetery may have been built as a "city of the dead" but its greatest importance now is as a haven for life.

That's the end of this tour around Arnos Vale but your exploration doesn't have to end here as the following walk begins at the Roman Catholic cemetery next door. Pass through the gates and turn right and you will be there after a very short walk.

Walk Eleven
Brislington

Brislington

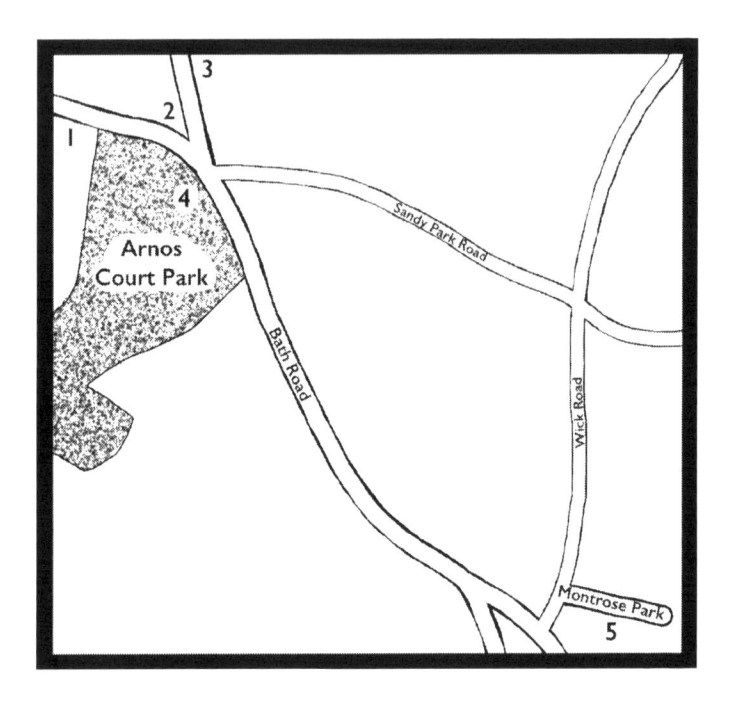

Although the area is best known as being home to Arnos Vale Cemetery, Brislington has had a rich and fascinating history of its own and was, for a long time, part of a vast estate which stretched for miles beyond the Bristol boundary.

Most of this walk is very straightforward but does weave around very busy roads. The final stop on the tour requires quite a climb up a hill so is probably best reserved only for the intrepid.

On this walk there will be, among other things, stories of a championship boxer, a dead nun who was bricked up behind a wall and one of the most sensationally gruesome murders the city has ever seen…

This walk begins at Holy Souls Catholic Cemetery. The gates are open on most days from 10am to 4pm.

1. Dixie Brown

Although it's often overlooked by visitors to Brislington in favour of Arnos Vale Cemetery, Holy Souls Cemetery is a quiet and atmospheric burial ground and really worth having a look around in conjunction with its famous neighbour. Its rows of uniform graves are strikingly sombre and the plot of land has a slight air of tumbledown neglect.

Built as a Catholic alternative to the Anglican and Nonconformist Arnos Vale, Holy Souls was established in 1856 and soon afterwards began filling with the bodies of Bristol's departed Catholics. By the 1850s, almost every graveyard in the city was full and new cemeteries had to be built farther afield from the bustling centre.

Of all the people interred at Holy Souls, few can boast of having lived as fascinating a life as Dixie Brown.

He was born Anthony George Charles on the 27th of June, 1900 in Castries, St. Lucia and his extraordinary body strength meant that, as a young teenager, he was sent to work on digging the Panama Canal.

It was through this work that he was able to save up enough money to move to Cardiff in 1919. He soon found employment as a bare-knuckle boxer, travelling Britain with various sideshows before he came to Bristol in 1923. It was there he found regular work as a conventional boxer in the classes of welterweight and middleweight.

Despite being popular and acclaimed throughout Bristol, Anthony George Charles, who was now working under the professional name of Dixie Brown, was not permitted to compete in any national championships as they were operated under colour-bars which prevented the Caribbean man from entry.

In the 1930s he was blinded in a fight. Friends, family and fans of the boxer paid for him to travel to Lourdes, France in the hope that the place of pilgrimage would restore his sight but unfortunately no such miracle occurred. He returned to Britain and never regained his vision.

When he died in 1957 he was survived by his wife, their nine children and thirty grandchildren. He was remembered as both a spectacular fighter and a much respected resident of Knowle West, where he lived out the last of his years.

After leaving the cemetery, turn right and follow the road until you come level with Sainsbury's car park. You should be able to see a large stone arch near the turning onto Bloomfield Road.

2. The Triumphal Arch

Standing alone on an island amidst a complex of roads in Brislington, the "Triumphal Arch" seems almost lost and out of place, but this attractive Bath stone gateway was once the entrance to a vast estate which has now been lost forever.

The estate belonged to businessman William Reeve, who had made his fortune through copper smelting at Crew's Hole, near St George in Bristol. The archway was intended to wow visitors to his property and to also provide an air of civic pride, by depicting four important figures in the city's history which can be found in the alcoves on either side of the structure.

The arch was built in 1760, soon after Reeves bought a huge plot of land in the area - when it was all open fields on the outskirts of the city. The original figures were also built at this time but were removed in 1898 when they had become so weathered that almost no features remained on them.

The alcoves remained empty until 1994, when sculptor Susan Dring was tasked with making depictions of the four men, and these are the statuettes which adorn the arch to this day.

The figures represent Edward I, who was gifted the entire town of Bristol in 1254 as part of his wedding celebrations when he was only 15 years old. On the same side, his grandson, Edward III can be found, he gave Bristol its royal charter in 1373, which set out certain rights for the people of the city and established it as a county in its own right.

On the reverse there are depictions of Bishop Geoffrey de Montbray, who was an adviser to William the Conqueror and played an important role in founding Bristol Castle, while the designer of the castle's keep, Robert Fitzroy can be found beside him. Incidentally, the keep designed by Fitzroy is one of the few pieces of the castle to still exist (though in ruins) and can be seen in Castle Park on the Galleries shopping centre side.

The entire gateway was moved in 1912 to allow for road expansion, but it was moved only a little distance, which explains why it now has such an incongruous home on a traffic island, but it remains a remarkably well preserved piece of Bristol history.

We're not finished with William Reeve just yet. Head towards the nearby Sainsbury's car park. In it you will find a rather strange looking black castle which now serves as a steakhouse and pub.

3. The Black Castle

Many people who visit the Brislington branch of Sainsbury's and notice the curious black castle assume that it must be a purpose built medieval theme-pub which has opened in recent years, but this castle - or rather, castle folly - was actually completed in 1755.

Although it's often described as an eyesore, it's rather fondly regarded by locals as a unique curio from history. It's believed to have been one of the first buildings constructed on the estate of William Reeve and likely served many uses, the primary of which was stables for horses.

It was not uncommon at the time to inject an air of whimsy into buildings which served functional purposes and the black castle was probably intended to be a lightly comical extravagance. Aside from stabling horses it probably served as laundry rooms and possibly housing for the workers on the estate.

The castle's colour is evidence of a commendable attempt at reusing waste. William Reeve owned a copper smelting factory and one of the by-products was a black slag that served little purpose after the copper ore had been separated from it. Usually this would be discarded as industrial waste, but Reeve obviously saw some use for it as a building product and constructed his castle folly from it.

The estate is now long gone, lost under concrete and tarmac, but the Black Castle (also known as Arno's Castle) continues to befuddle visitors to Brislington Sainsbury's car park and will continue to do so for generations.

Return towards the Triumphal Arch. From there you will see the Arnos Manor Hotel on the opposite side of the road. This is the next stop on this walk.

4. The Arnos Manor Hotel Ghost

The Arnos Manor Hotel in Brislington is a charming, cosy hotel away from the city centre, which enjoys a reputation as an offbeat location for a less traditional stay in Bristol. However, for years there have been reports that something is amiss within the walls of this lovely old building.

The hotel was originally built as a house for William Reeve and his family in 1760 and was one of the largest homes in the city at the time - so large that it was even built with its own private chapel, so that the Reeve family and their many servants would not have to leave the estate even for church services.

The house was sold in 1774 and in 1851 it was extended to the rear and began operating as a convent - the chapel was used as a school for girls in the area - and a large portion of the grounds was taken over by the ever expanding Arnos Vale Cemetery.

Arnos Vale Manor is perhaps best known for a curious and frightening tale from this period. It is said that a nun who lived at the convent in the 19th century became pregnant after a scandalous relationship with a local man and rather than face the judgemental ire of her convent sisters, decided to take her own life.

The nuns at Arnos Manor did not want this scandal to become public knowledge, so they bricked the corpse of the woman behind a false wall in one of the rooms. For many decades this story was regarded as little more than a spooky legend - especially as nuns being buried behind walls is a surprisingly common trope in ghost stories - but the rumours seemed to be validated in the 1940s.

It's claimed that during WWII a German bomb caused some minor damage to the manor and workers were sent in to do repairs. When demolishing part of the wall, they uncovered the skeletal remains of a woman which had been hidden away for almost a century. For whatever reason, the workers decided that it would be best just to bury the bones on the property.

The truth of this story is hard to ascertain. The problem with ghost stories is that so often there is a kernel of truth behind them, but one that gets elaborated on so completely that it becomes impossible to tell reality from fiction, but since the 1940s it's been said that the nun has haunted Arnos Manor Hotel.

Presumably she was at peace behind the bricked up wall, because ever since her remains were reburied she has been sighted around the hotel, sometimes climbing staircases that no longer exist, filling bathtubs with water, speaking in a disembodied voice to fearful visitors and perhaps most alarmingly, sitting on the chests of people while they sleep so that they cannot breathe.

Whatever the truth of the matter, the Arnos Manor ghost has proven to be quite a draw, with room 160 - which is said to be the focus of the paranormal activity - frequently requested by guests to the hotel.

It's a bit of a trek to the next location, but it's well worth it if you're interested in true crime! Follow the Bath Road up the hill and away from Arnos Vale and bear left when the road forks in two. Take the third left turning onto Wick Road and then the first right onto Montrose Park.

5. The Brislington Hatchet Murder

Montrose Park is a pretty and quiet residential street, but in 1923 it was the scene of a gruesome murder which would become a media sensation (and possibly the inspiration behind an Alfred Hitchcock classic).

In a house along this terrace, George Cooper Jnr. bludgeoned his own father to death with a hatchet, a crime which would lead to him serving only seven years in prison and would win him sympathy across the country.

George Cooper Snr. was a notorious womaniser and an abusive husband. At the time of his death it's believed that he was having multiple affairs with women, mostly in Bedminster where he worked as a pattern maker alongside his son. George Snr. was not averse to physical abuse and was said to have routinely beaten his wife, sometimes even dragging her by her hair, George Jnr. was frequently struck by his father too.

By 1923, George Cooper Snr. was 59 years old, his wife Louisa, 57 and their son George was 37. George Jnr. had married a couple of years earlier and had moved his wife into his family home and the couple soon welcomed a child - a boy, confusingly also called George.

George Jnr.'s wife was expecting a second child in September of that year and went to stay with her mother until the baby was born. It was during this time that George murdered his father.

At the trial both George Jnr. and his mother claimed that George Snr. had returned from work in a fit of rage. To steady his nerves after a physical fight with his father, George went to the family's piano to play music and it was then that he saw his father enter the room brandishing an axe with the intent of bludgeoning his son with the handle.

George Jnr. described being taken by a fierce temper and wrestling the axe from his father's hands. The last thing he claimed to remember was seeing a black and red mist descend before his eyes, and the next thing he knew, he was standing over the remains of his father.

What he and his mother did next caused their story to become a national media sensation. They buried his body beneath the floorboards of their living room and slid the piano over his untimely grave.

When George Snr. failed to show up for work, his son and wife played up rumours that he had eloped with one of his many mistresses. At Christmas of that year, the pair threw a house party for their neighbours and the guests sang and revelled around the piano, completely unaware that they were literally dancing on the dead man's grave.

The stress of the deception clearly took its toll on George Jnr., because in January of 1924 he confessed the crime to a friend - a retired police officer - who immediately reported it to the local constabulary. By the time the police came to arrest George they had already detained his mother.

The trial drew journalists from around Britain and salacious reporting on the details of the murder kept the country gripped for days. However, the mood of the nation was largely sympathetic to George and his mother and this was reflected in their sentencing.

George Jnr. was sentenced to seven years imprisonment, Louisa was found guilty of hiding the body but did not serve any time at all. The general mood seemed to be that they had rid Bristol of a ghastly man and the world was better off without George Cooper Snr. in it.

In 1929, Patrick Hamilton published his play *Rope*, which was made into a film by Alfred Hitchcock in 1948. Although it's often claimed that Hamilton's inspiration for his stage play was the 1924 murder of Bobby Franks by Nathan Leopold and Richard Loeb, the story itself, which concerns a murderous duo hosting a party for friends while the corpse of a murdered man is hidden nearby, is believed to have at least been partly inspired by the Brislington hatchet murder.

That is the end of this walk. I hope you've enjoyed this exploration of one of the under-appreciated quarters of our city.

Walk Twelve
Ashton Court

Ashton Court

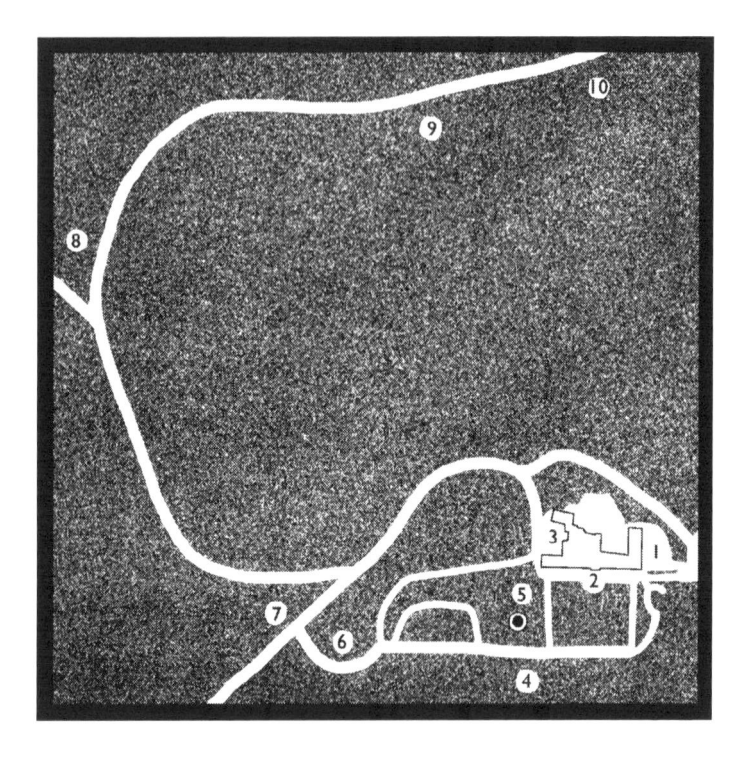

Ashton Court Estate is actually located in Somerset, but it's owned and operated by Bristol City Council, so I feel fully at liberty to feature it here!

It is without a doubt, my favourite park in what I'm going to refer to in this chapter as the "Bristol area", which is why I saved this for the final walk of the book.

This is a moderately difficult walk. The route I will guide you through consists entirely of robust tarmac walkways, but the section after stop number 8 requires quite a steep climb.

I hope that this adventure inspires not just a better understanding of this wonderful green space, but a lovely day out too. So pack a picnic and prepare to encounter a headless horseman, a charismatic conman and hoard of treasure which may still be buried beneath the estate…

This walk begins at Ashton Court mansion. I suggest a coffee at the east side of the house in the section which used to be stables for horses before we begin this tour!

1. The Frankenstein House

The strange profusion of architectural styles which make up the Ashton Court mansion have led some people to claim that the building is hard to love. However, the almost nonsensical combination of designs have also allowed it to become a sort of time capsule, telling the stories of its enormous history.

There has been a manor house on this spot in some form since the 11th century and what may be left of that building (if anything) is believed to be wedged into the centre of the current mansion on all sides.

In its first few centuries of existence it seems that most of the work carried out on the house were cosmetic alterations or general upkeep of the old building. In 1541 the house was bought by John Smyth - and his family would be associated with the house until 1946, with the death of the last of the Smyth lineage.

John Smyth was the first to make significant alterations to the house but many of these were subsequently demolished by his son, Thomas.

John was rumoured to be something of a tyrant who ran the house with a disregard for his servants, which was deemed monstrous even for the age. It's said that when Queen Elizabeth I came to visit Bristol in 1574 she was persuaded by her advisors not to stay at Ashton Court, such was his perceived villainy.

Thomas Smyth took over the house in 1609 and it's him who first radically changed the layout of the property. It can be hard to ascertain from the outside just what a garbled maze of interlocking wings the whole structure consists of, but this confusing web is mostly down to his design ideas.

Thomas seems to have never met a European architectural style he did not like and gleefully threw several all together in his rebuilding of the mansion, sometimes incorporating several into the same aspect.

Most of the subsequent generations have attempted to cover up the worst of these excesses but it has not always been successful. In the 1800s, Sir John Smyth attempted to bring a sense of grandeur to the southern side of the building by commissioning the mansion's most notable feature - the long facade on either side of a 16th century gatehouse - but this did not help matters much as it was designed to be completely asymmetrical with different window styles applied to each half.

Sir John Smyth never married and he became the last of the direct line of the Smyth family to reside in the house, it passed through various cousins and nieces and began to look worse for wear.

With the death of Esme Smyth in 1946 the house was in such a sorry state that the council decided to buy it along with the 850 acre estate it sits within. Shortly afterwards it was opened as a public park.

Ashton Court Estate is now one of the most popular in the Bristol area, and its bizarre Frankenstein's Monster of a house is a much loved oddity among the people of the city.

Stay where you are for the next one. Look up at the original Tudor gatehouse and the narrow windows which can be found close to the roof.

2. Ashton Court Ghosts

No old mansion worth its salt should be without a resident ghost - and Ashton Court (and its surrounding estate) can boast three of them - two of which are truly strange and terrifying.

The grey lady is the apparition most commonly reported and is usually seen peering down from an upstairs window of the south wing's gatehouse.

She may have been sighted for over a century and there has been a great deal of speculation as to who she could be. A popular theory is that she represents a maid who was locked away in an upper room of the house as a punishment and either perished from starvation or flung herself to her death.

As with many ghost stories, there is not a shred of evidence to support the claim that anybody died in such a manner at Ashton Court.

Another ghost is said to haunt the grounds and appears only on moonlit nights. It is the frightful ghost of a headless horseman, riding a gigantic black steed across the open fields. It's not known quite when this story originated but it's a curious detail that throughout Britain almost all headless ghosts are usually those of royalty or aristocracy.

One suggestion is that he is the ghost of Thomas Smyth, the former owner of the house who has come to guard the hoard of treasure he and his manservant buried on the estate (more on that story later on this walk) but how this ghost managed to lose his head is a mystery.

The third apparition may be even more chilling (if that were possible) and may not be a ghost at all but a terrifying beast. It's an enormous black dog, sometimes seen with glowing eyes and strangely, backwards facing feet.

The idea of devil hounds roaming the English countryside is a centuries old fear and in various parts of the country the dog is known as the barguest, shuck, grim or gytrash and is almost always seen as a portent of death, either for the witness or somebody they know. However, in Somerset, (where most of Ashton Court is actually situated) it is often called the Gurt Dog and not only behaves benevolently but has been known to guide lost travellers to safety.

Continue around the house to the west wing (the bright yellow side) this entrance is where something rather strange happened in the middle of the night in 1852.

3. The Ashton Court Fraud

In the early hours of an October night in 1852, a knock came at the door of Ashton Court mansion. Stepping into the house, the man announced that he was Sir Richard Smyth, the eldest son of Sir Hugh Smyth and the rightful heir of the estate.

Richard was not an unreasonable man, so he insisted that the residents of the house and their servants had a few hours before he forced them off his property.

Understandably, this news came as quite a shock to the house's inhabitants. With the death of the final man in the Smyth bloodline, the house was in the possession of a cousin - Greville Smyth, who had dutifully changed his surname from Upton after inheriting the property. If it could be proven that this gentleman was truly the long-lost son of Hugh Smyth, the house and its estate - as well as the substantial payments of over £25,000 the surrounding farmland earned - would all be rightfully his.

Unsurprisingly, he was sent away from the house but returned the following morning with a solicitor. He presented Greville with a will which he claimed had been signed by Hugh Smyth and bequeathed his son his entire fortune.

While Greville set about securing a case for himself, Richard went to tenant farmers and promised he would offer them reduced rents if they vouched for his authenticity. Slowly the handsome and convincing man began to win support across the city.

The trial began in early 1853 and was reported around the world. There is something about upending the British class system which has a universal appeal and the story made front page headlines for days.

One of the most sensational moments came when an expert in forgeries revealed his conclusion on the will that Richard had presented at the mansion. In his opinion the paper was new and not over thirty years old as it would have to have been for the late Sir Hugh Smyth to have signed it. Even more damning, he believed the signature to be a forgery.

The most bizarre incident happened the following day. Clearly with his back against the wall and nowhere else to turn, the man alleging to be Sir Richard Smyth produced a clipped ponytail from his pocket. Only true heirs of the Smyth fortune were born with a ponytail, claimed Richard, and the hair had been clipped from his eldest son on the day of his birth.

Shockingly, this did not convince the magistrate and as the case in favour of Richard Smyth unravelled, so did the full story of the man behind the fraud.

Tom Provis was a horse thief and forger, who had spent the previous years travelling the country and giving lectures at universities and claiming to be a doctor, despite having no qualifications whatsoever.

Provis was eventually found guilty and was sentenced to twenty years transportation. However, the man was so convincing that many continued to believe his story, including some members of the Smyth family who carried on writing to him until he died in 1855, just two years into his sentence.

In a brutal age when it was hard to survive as a poor man it's hard not to have some sympathy for Tom Provis. A fiendish deception had left a man in tatters and Ashton Court would remain in the hands of the Smyth family for almost a hundred more years.

Follow the edge of the house back to the southern facade and then head down either of the two paths which run at either side of the grand lawn until you reach a broader path. Head right and after going down a few steps you should be able to spot a cluster of stones among the grass. Most of them have visible engravings of names. This our next stop on the walk.

4. The Pet Cemetery

American author and two-time Pulitzer Prize winner David McCullough famously once said "nobody ever lived in the past" - because at whatever time in history somebody was alive, they were living in what was for them, the modern day.

Sometimes it can feel as if people in history lived such different lives that it can be hard to relate to them, but every so often they leave behind something poignant and human that suddenly renders them as being very real.

The pet cemetery in Ashton Court is such a relic. It's a collection of about forty headstones (there may be more but they have been lost to time) with each one marking the resting place of one of the family's beloved pets.

Because some of the stones have become so worn with time it isn't clear when the first animal was buried here, but it was probably sometime in the mid 19th century, when pet cemeteries became popular in Britain, but the Smyth family could well have been burying departed pets on this spot much earlier.

Of the pets buried in the cemetery, the majority are thought to have been dogs, as consecutive members of the Smyth family were known to keep them, but there is at least one monkey known to be underground. Monkeys became a brief fad as pets in Britain and France from the 1870s onward.

The cemetery would once have been in the dappled shade of a redwood tree but the tree was removed during alterations to the grounds in 2010. It's now an unusual but touching memorial to the non-human residents of Ashton Court estate and also a reminder that the bond between people and their companions is as timeless as it is unbreakable.

On the opposite side of the path to the pet cemetery, there is an embankment. Steps will lead you up to a garden which is perpetually shaded by enormous redwood trees.

5. Humphry Repton

It's often said that the grounds of Ashton Court were designed by "the last great landscape designer of the 18th century" and while this is true, it omits the fact that the designer in question, Humphry Repton, didn't actually visit the estate until 1802.

Although often seen as a less significant landscaper to Capability Brown, Repton had an enormous impact on the way in which grand gardens are laid out and the 850 acres of Ashton Court remain testament to his skilled eye for working with nature.

Repton was born in Bury St Edmunds in 1752 and it was assumed he would follow his father into a career in finance. His father had been a tax collector but had started his own business dealing with private transport companies. At a young age, Humphry was sent to the Netherlands to learn Dutch, a vitally important skill of the age as the Netherlands led the world in international trade.

Young Repton, however, had much more of an interest in art, which was nurtured by the Dutch family he was staying with. After he returned to England, he spent several years in different jobs but none of them worked out well for him and he failed to find much financial success. It wasn't until 1788 that he first tried his hand at landscape gardening.

Before Capability Brown, the tradition for gardening had been one of uniformed symmetry. The Tudors in particular were especially fond of manicured grounds, with expertly trimmed knot gardens and occasional topiary, but by the early 1700s this style was beginning to look rather unfashionable. The only problem was that nobody had really come up with an idea of what should replace it.

Brown's concept was to create much less formal, natural spaces. He introduced flowing waterways and meandering pathways which would take people on a journey through the grounds. He would obscure certain views with rows of trees so that they could be revealed from a prime location and exposed elements of the surrounding environment by removing woodlands.

Brown died in 1783, so Repton was in a prime position to become his successor, and that's precisely what happened, with Repton's grand creations winning immediate admirers and his designs in great demand. Unlike Brown, who designed his landscapes with maps and diagrams, Repton took a more artistic approach, creating beautiful portfolios known as his Red Books which were filled with watercolour paintings and "before and after" images of how the gardens would look.

He never produced a Red Book for Ashton Court but he did have many ideas for how it should be laid out. He extended an existing "ha-ha" - a ditch which separated the edge of the grounds from the land used for grazing cattle - so that there would be an unbroken view from the house but the animals would not be able to enter the grounds.

Beyond that, he laid out the trails which would guide visitors through a choice of several adventures, leading through dense forests or over high hills which overlooked the city. In a sunken garden on the west of the house he suggested an ornamental pond. This area has now been dominated by giant sequoias which were planted in 1900 and are some of the largest trees to be found in the Bristol area.

Repton never made the same kind of fortune as Brown but he became comfortably well off from his designs. As well as being seen as the successor to Capability, he is also credited with introducing the 19th century to a style of gardening that, though incredibly labour intensive and expensive, looked as if it could feasibly have grown by itself.

The landscape of Ashton Court is enjoyed by thousands of visitors each year, as are his other designs at Blaise Castle and Royal Fort in Bristol. He remains one of Britain's most admired - and copied gardeners.

Return to the path and follow the avenue of trees away from the house and past a beautiful rose garden on your right. Go through the gate, and where the path splits, follow it to the left into an opening through shrubbery to a dark but small patch of woodland. On your right there will be a small stone building. This is the ice house and the next stop on this walk.

6. The Ice House

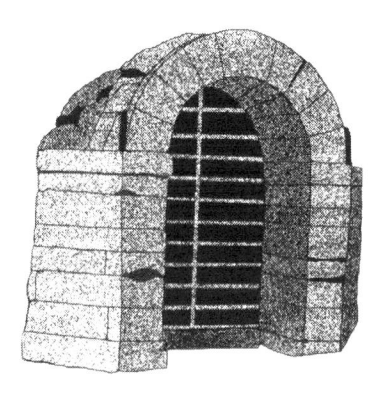

Hidden away in a small scrap of woodland and looking not unlike an igloo (a design choice which may well be intentional) is the Ashton Court ice house.

It's not known exactly when it was built but plans of the land establish it was constructed sometime towards the late 18th or early 19th century, which would suggest it was one of the final alterations to the estate made by Sir John Hugh Smyth and his wife Elizabeth. This was also about the same time that ice houses became popular throughout Britain.

During the Georgian era these underground cellars became very fashionable among the social elite. Having ice during the summer months was seen as the height of sophistication as it took such extraordinary effort to get it. This ice was used for cooling drinks but also making ice creams and sorbets.

The ice would have been collected throughout the winter, and if the season was cold enough, it would even be prepared in large scale ice trays. However, if it had been a particularly mild winter, the ice could be delivered from Scotland or even Scandinavia. Unsurprisingly, this option was prohibitively expensive.

The ice would be tightly bound in cloths and stacked in piles underground where it could potentially last almost indefinitely, even if the summer was a particularly warm one. The simplicity of this design is such that if you stand by the entrance, you can often feel cold drafts billowing from the dark opening.

The staircase that can be seen through the entrance goes down about 12 metres. Its placement away from the house may seem rather strange but this was because it needed to be built in a shaded area of the estate and on ground which was easy to dig through. It also had the benefit that ice could be brought immediately to picnickers who were enjoying the grounds nearby.

The ice house is an intriguing curiosity for those who find themselves in this seldom visited corner of the estate and is a rare example of this type of building to be found in Britain today.

Continue following the path through the woods until you are overlooking a gigantic field.

7. Buried Treasure

The grounds of Ashton Court are enjoyed by hundreds of thousands of visitors each year but what few people seem to be aware of is the fact that hidden somewhere on the vast estate there may be a hoard of treasure which has remained lost for centuries.

With the outbreak of the English Civil War in 1642 there was a fear among the upper classes that the social hierarchy of England would be upended in the event of a victory by the Parliamentarians. Moreover, there had been word that skirmishes across the country had led to country houses being pillaged for their goods. As war became an inevitability, it seems the master of the house took drastic measures to protect his fortune.

Thomas Smyth is said to have asked his manservant to bury the entirety of the family's silver to prevent it from being stolen. The location of this burial was a closely guarded secret known only to him and his steward.

Later that year Thomas Smyth unexpectedly died, as did his manservant, and the secret of the location of the treasure was buried with them.

This treasure hoard, possibly amounting to millions in today's money, has been searched for over the centuries, but not a single piece of silver has ever been found. The most recent large-scale search for the family's fortune came in the 1930s when Esme Smyth - who would be the last in the line of Smyth's to own Ashton Court Estate - conducted a survey of possible locations the treasure could be buried.

The search proved futile, and poor Esme, who was already close to financial ruin due to Ashton Court Manor being in such a state of disarray, resorted to prying open the family's tomb in search of a gold ring one of her ancestors had been rumoured to be buried with.

Could there be any truth to the tale of the lost treasure? Possibly. It was not unheard of for people in possession of vast fortunes to resort to such measures following the outbreak of war. There is a chance that buried somewhere beneath the enormous estate there is a hoard of unimaginable treasures just waiting to be found!

Continue into the large field and follow the path to the right. Take the first left and head all the way to the edge of a steep hill at the corner of the fallow deer park.

8. The Deer Parks

Easily among the star attractions of Ashton Court are its two magnificent and gigantic deer parks (both have vast wooded areas, so are even larger than they initially appear). They offer a rare and important chance for urban dwellers to have a close encounter with some of Britain's largest native animals, but there is more to these parks than that of the visual splendour they add to the estate.

There are two deer parks in Ashton Court. The one by the entrance to the estate is home to a herd of red deer, while the other, by the large field which is host to the annual Balloon Fiesta, is home to fallow deer. While they are a welcome addition to the estate, it's astonishing to remember that these deer parks have been in continuous use since at least the 15th century.

In fact, there is bone evidence to suggest that deer may have been kept on this land even earlier - possibly even predating Ashton Court Estate entirely.

Deer were primarily kept for hunting and as a food source, but stags in particular have had a long association with nobility, being represented on coats of arms and family crests throughout the ages.

Access to both parks is permitted throughout most of the year, with gates to the fallow deer park in the redwood forest and ones to the red deer found at the top and lower edges of the park. The only time the gates are closed is during rutting season, (where stags take on each other in terrifying and sometimes brutal battles of strength) and shortly after fauns have been born.

If you look out across the red deer park from the position of the nearby car park you should be able to see ridges along a faraway hill. These are Saxon era drainage channels and are among the earliest examples of farming practices in the Bristol area. They date back to about 500 AD and may be evidence that the estate has been in constant use for over 1500 years.

Follow the path on the right, upwards until you come to a large stone head which overlooks the house. This head represents the giant Goram and is the next stop on our walk.

9. Bristol and Balloons

Ashton Court is probably best known across the country for its annual balloon fiesta. The event regularly draws crowds of over 100,000 people each day and is one of the largest festivals of its type in the world.

The fiesta was first held in 1979 and was the brainchild of Bedminster-based Cameron Balloons founder Don Cameron. His company is responsible for manufacturing balloons which have set and broken countless records in speed, height and endurance.

However, Ashton Court's association with balloons goes beyond a mere four days each August and the field which is overlooked by a stone head of the mythical giant Goram is host to hundreds of launches each year and on summer evenings Bristolians are occasionally treated to the magical sight of the skies over the city being filled with hot air balloons.

Despite the fiesta and modern-day launches, Bristol's love affair with ballooning actually goes back much further.

In 1810, balloonist and renowned pastry chef James Sadler drew crowds of thousands when he sailed over the city in a hot air balloon. Perhaps suspecting that this would not be enough of a spectacle, he brought a cat along with him which he dropped from the basket. The cat was equipped with a parachute, which successfully deployed, and caught by a physician who was watching the flight. The physician adopted the cat and named him "Balloon".

One of the very earliest flights over the city was in 1784 when a Mr Dinwiddle and Dr Parry raced one another in balloons which were launched from Bath. Dinwiddle was the first to make it to Bristol, landing safely near Troopers Hill. The place where he touched down is named in his honour as Air Balloon Road.

Continue up the hill. On your right you should see a rather forlorn and broken tree which is barely being held up by struts and has partially collapsed. This is the final stop on this walk.

10. The Domesday Oak

The Domesday Oak in Ashton Court is believed to be one of the oldest trees in the entire Bristol area. It has stood on the side of a hill for over 700 years and has been a silent witness to the city's extraordinary history.

When it was a mere acorn, Bristol was a small but important city on the River Avon, and when it was a sapling, it had first established itself as a port of significance.

As a young sprig of a tree, Bristol was awarded a charter by King Edward III which established the town as a county and gave the townspeople certain rights which were exclusive to them.

When the Domesday Oak first bore acorns, Bristol was being ravaged by a series of plagues which would kill over half of its population, and by the time Henry VIII came to the throne, it was now overlooking the third largest city in the country.

When Queen Elizabeth I visited the city in 1574, the tree was a handsome gent and Bristol was second only to London in importance to international trade and by the time Queen Victoria was our monarch, the city was an industrial powerhouse and the tree was blowing in winds which were thick with dark smog.

The Domesday Oak first started to show signs of age with the outbreak of WW1, when the grounds of Ashton Court were used for training conscripted soldiers in trench warfare and when bombs dropped upon the city in 1940, the tree was a grand old man and heaving beneath its own weight.

By the turn of the millennium the oak was very aged indeed and soon afterwards developed a crack. In 2011 support struts were added to the branches, but these were only partially successful and the tree broke in half soon afterwards.

Now it rests broken but surviving. The Domesday Oak may be heaving its last breaths but the city it has overlooked for centuries will continue to go on. Like the tree itself, it is a rare and wonderful treasure.

That is the end of this walk and the end of this book. I really hope you've enjoyed this adventure with me.

About the Author

Charlie Revelle-Smith was born in Essex and raised in Cornwall but in the year 2000, he moved to Bristol to study English and Sociology at the University of the West of England.

He learned a lot over those three years at university, most significantly, how much he loved his adopted home.

Now regarding himself as a "Naturalised Bristolian" Charlie spends a good portion of his life wandering the streets of Bristol, often accompanied by his dog Reggie, in search of oddities for his popular Twitter feed and Instagram account @WeirdBristol, which documents the lesser known and hidden history of the city.

The *Weird Bristol* book became Charlie's first non-fiction book after writing several successful novels (and a few unsuccessful ones!) Many of his novels are historic mysteries, mostly set during the Victorian era and early 20th century, but from 2015-18 he published *The Bristol Murders* series which are set in contemporary Bristol.

More Weird Bristol is the second book in the *Weird Bristol* trilogy. The third title, *Further Weird Bristol* will be published in 2020.

Printed in Great Britain
by Amazon